The Adventures
of a Romantic

The Adventures of a Romantic

A Life Story

by

Bernard Jay

Bernard Jay
in association with
Logaston Press

BERNARD JAY
in association with
LOGASTON PRESS
Little Logaston, Logaston,
Woonton, Almeley, Herefordshire HR3 6QH

First published by Bernard Jay & Logaston Press 1998

ISBN 1 873827 50 4

Set in Times by Logaston Press
and printed in Great Britain by
The Cromwell Press, Trowbridge, Wilts

*Front Cover: Bernard Jay holding a photograph of his younger
self—shortly after he had enlisted in the Grenadier Guards
Rear Cover: Transport Platoon, 3rd Battalion Grenadier Guards*

Contents

To Ellis and Kay

Acknowledgements

I wish to especially thank those people who have encouraged me to write this book, and those who have helped me check information and details, notably Messrs. Jim and Sid Davies of Winforton, Herefordshire; Bernard Kindred for his encouragement; Mrs. Yvonne Lloyd Dudley, Llandeilo's Librarian; Mr. 'Matty' Hayes, ex-Sgt. Grenadier Guards; and ex-Sgt. George Webb, also ex-Grenadier Guards; Mr. and Mrs. Alexis & Carmen Querales together with Brian Byron for the map of Venezuela; and Dr. Ian Cameron, now deceased, for drawings of birds on the Algarve. Thanks must also go to Andy Johnson of Logaston Press for advice and help in ensuring this story saw the light of day.

Note

Max, Vincent's son (see p.68) would like any ex-Grenadier who knew Vincent to get in touch with him. Max's home address is: 95 Stoney Lane, Bloxwich, Walsall, West Midlands WR3 3RE. Tel: 01922 479440. I would like to hear from the other four comrades who survived the bombing but were badly wounded; I can be contacted via Logaston Press.

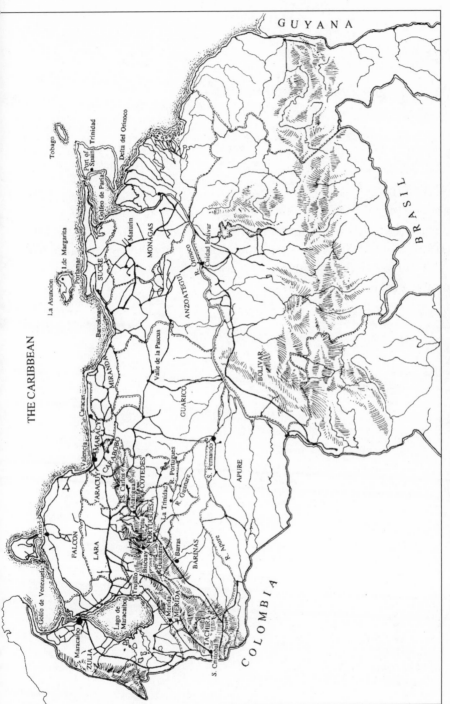

Map of Venezuela showing principal places and those mentioned in the text

1
Winforton

Winforton is situated on the A438 to the north-west of the city of Hereford, halfway between the villages of Willersley and Whitney-on-Wye and seven miles from the Welsh border town of Hay-on-Wye, now internationally known as the book centre of the world. It is where I was born at Nicholas Farm about midnight on January 26, 1920. I say about midnight because my mother always told me that my birthday was on the 26th, but my birth certificate says the 27th. I don't suppose my poor old Mother knew what day it was anyway. I didn't! I was the first of three children and was a continual source of worry to my parents ever after.

Winforton played a significant role in the 1939/1945 war—apart from me being one of its sons I mean—as the village squire, Professor Thomas Merton, for whom not enough credit has ever been given, conceived the idea with Barnes Wallace of the bouncing bomb by watching school boys skimming stones on the river Wye. The allies were trying to bomb the Moehne Dam and the bombs were gliding away from it, instead of bouncing towards it. The consequence of their work was that on the 16/17 May 1943 the dam was breached when a rectangular wedge of 250 ft in width by 112 ft deep in a 50 ft thick wall was achieved and 45,000 cubic feet of masonry removed. Apart from 476 German dead and 69 missing, 590 foreign workers dead and 146 missing for which the raid was not intended, both the Moehne and the Eder dams were emptied; the Mittelland Canal was severely disrupted; the storage power station was flooded; the main railway line between Kassell and Hagen was destroyed and the city of Kassell was submerged 40 miles down-stream. Bridges around for miles were destroyed and mud swept over the whole area and disrupted the war machine for months. Harvests were ruined. Four million inhabitants had their water supply cut. Hundreds of thousands of frantically required personnel were needed to repair the communications and hydro-electric plants were put out of action, but the Germans had the Moehne in working order by the end of September 1943, and the dam was completely restored by August 1944. Unfortunately there was a debit side to the operation as well; 8 of our planes were lost and 55 airmen killed. Incidentally, Thomas Merton was Chairman of the Tribunal of Scientific Advisers to the Ministry of Supply, and it was he who both realised that Barnes Wallis was one of the greatest engineers of all time when others were not prepared to listen to him, and helped secure his subsequent knighthood.

The Second World War even came to little Winforton, not because of the Professor, but because someone left the lights on at Castleton Farm—it would be a farmer, wouldn't it!—some of them lived in cloud cuckoo land and were quite unaware that there was a war on. The Jerries dropped a string of bombs along the river Wye bank doing no harm to anyone except the fish, especially the salmon that turned round in shock and went back to the Bristol Channel where they remained for the next two years, scared of coming up the river Wye. They say some of the bombs are still in the ground, unexploded.

Nicholas Farm was a smallholding of roughly 20 acres spread all over the place, with a couple of horses, some few dairy cattle and sheep of indeterminate breed, free range poultry including ducks, geese, turkeys and chickens that mostly looked after themselves, and tasted the better for it. Occasionally mother threw out some corn for them, but we had to be economical with it as in those days farmers did not cultivate maize and it cost 6/- a cwt (30p) which was a lot of money in the 1920s. A farm labourer worked six days a week for £1, and after paying his employer 2/6d (12.5p) rent for his cottage was left with 17/6d (87.5p) on which to clothe and feed his

2

family of wife and four children. (There was no TV or electricity so he had to find something to do!) For lighting in our little black and white farmhouse we used a paraffin lamp and candles in the bedrooms. There was no indoor toilet, so that whilst there was a chamber pot under the bed, we otherwise had to get dressed—there was no money for dressing gowns—light the lantern and go down to the privvy at the bottom of the garden, usually accompanied by Mum or Dad. There was no toilet paper so we used to cut the *Hereford Times* into minute sized squares and hang the paper on a nail. Posh, pink toilet paper did not exist for us.

For as long as I can remember, even before going to school, our lives revolved around the Apostolic Church in Hay-on-Wye and 'meetings' at home where friends and relatives, such as Uncle Leonard and Aunt Emily, Dad's sister and brother-in-law from Pen-tri-coed Farm, about five miles away in Wales, used to come down with their pony and trap through all weathers and pick up Tom Lawrence, who had a smallholding at Woodseaves, on the way. Usually the 'meetings' would last a couple of hours during which time there would be prayers, hymns and testimonies, and little Dad—he was about 5 feet tall (or short) and weighed about 7 stones, would play the peddle organ by ear. Before the folks departed Mother always made pots of tea and produced a large golden brown cake, which she had baked the previous evening ready for the 'meeting'. Mother always baked her own bread and cakes which were the envy of people for miles around, in the large oven built into the wall which was part of the cooking range in a not too spacious kitchen.

On Sundays we went by trap to the Apostolic Church in Hay-on-Wye, drawn by our bay mare which did the seven miles in roughly an hour, having to cross the toll bridge at Whitney-on-Wye where the charge for crossing the bridge was 4d for the pony and trap, plus 1d for each passenger—Sunday was an expensive day. We spent the whole day there with the morning service, Sunday School and the evening service. The ladies brought sandwiches and cakes and made tea in the vestry so that some of us, including the

Grennows from Llanigon in the Black Mountains—they were farmers too—remained in church the whole day, and it became more of a social gathering as well as a day of worship. During the winter there was always the stove that burned coke in the middle of the room. There was no such thing as oil-fired central heating, or electricity for that matter, only gas. It was a long day for us children, but there were others there, so we were able to pass the time although no games were allowed. The Sabbath was strictly observed in every respect, and in any case we were wearing our Sunday best; our best suits and dresses for Sundays only, so how could we play games? Public houses, by the way, were closed on Sundays and no dancing was allowed. There was always a Sunday School outing to Barry for the children, but I suppose because we couldn't usually afford it, I can only remember going once. I do recall the story of a farmer who, after attending church, decided to risk it and get on with the hay-making, hoping no one would see him. No sooner had he and his two sons started to turn the hay than there was a loud clap of thunder, at which the father said: 'It's no good boys, He has seen us, let's go home.'

On our return journey we bedded down on the floor of the trap, waking up and not knowing where we were when we arrived home. Our parents had to milk the few cows that we had before going to church and again on returning home. Dad, incidentally, used to walk the seven miles if there was no other way of getting there; his faith was more important to him than anything else. We never had a wireless or newspaper in our house, except the weekly *Hereford Times*, because our parents did not approve of them and did not wish our minds to be contaminated with worldly affairs, but then they were completely out of touch. During the 1914-18 war Dad was a conscientious objector and spent two years in Liverpool goal and Wormwood Scrubs where Fenner Brockway was his close companion. The first he must have known of the war was when he received his call-up papers which were forthwith ignored, and he awaited the eventual arrival of the local copper. My father was not a saint as some would suggest, but he was a good man. He

4

confessed during his later years that he dallied quite a lot before he got married, but don't we all, I said. He used to cycle 20 miles up into Wales to go and see a young lady every weekend. He seemed quite worried about it. He was that sort of person.

Our little school in the village of Winforton has since been converted into a private residence like so many others, and the children of the village have to go to Eardisley some four miles round the corner, but in the 1920s it was a thriving little school with about 30 children in attendance. The headmistress, and only teacher, was a Miss Williams from Wales. We used to call her Boombie because she bounced up and down. She lived in the school house attached to the school as in the case of most, alone. Freda Lloyd, whose family ran the village post office, and who was a teacher in Eardisley primary school, was Miss Williams's relief teacher and helped out on the infrequent occasions when 'Boombie' was indisposed. Miss Williams must have been a very kind and sympathetic teacher, because I cannot ever remember her caning anyone in the school; she may have sent us 'into the corner' on many occasion, but that was as far as the punishment went, apart from making us write out something a hundred times, which meant having to remain behind after school hours. I was an absolute dunce at school and as thick as two short planks—I think my mother must have dropped me from a great height onto the floor when I was born, from which I never completely recovered—and never seemed to fully comprehend anything that was being said; even when I attended school in the Army I had the same problem and really needed private tutoring, so it wasn't the fault of Miss Williams. Neither did I excel in sports, and we had plenty of opportunity because a Mr Roger Powell, a local farmer, kindly lent us a field near the school where we were allowed to play football and cricket, as well as rugby, the girls playing volley ball. But rugby was more like rough and tumble because we didn't know the rules and there was no P.E. Instructor in a school of our size. Scrums were more like a team wrestling match. We had one air-gun belonging to the school, so that on wet days we were allowed to use the Parish Hall for target practice. You were jolly lucky if you got in one solitary shot. The gun was eventually given to The Sun Inn as a memento. My chief sport was chasing a certain Frankie Gregg who was the same age as myself, and the chemistry exploded every time we were within sight of each other resulting in a real punch-up; we were like red rags to a bull. On several occasions Boombie made us stand in the corner on opposite sides of the classroom. Having been away from the area for so long I had wanted to meet him again on more favourable terms, but I understand the poor chap has passed on now.

We used to walk to school from Nicholas Farm across the common and down the narrow road, which was only about half a mile, but to me then it seemed more like 10 miles, especially as I used to give the pond a wide berth. When I was about 3 years old and playing on the common with some friends, Mrs Turner's gander from Goose Pool took a distinct dislike to me and flew at me with its enormous wings a-flapping and wrestled me to the ground, my forehead in its razor-like bill. If it hadn't been for my old friend Jim Davies, who was about seven years older than myself, I would have been a gonner. He came to my rescue and gathered me up in his arms delivering me, covered in blood, to my anguished mother. I still have the scar on my forehead 77 years on. Thereafter it was essential to take a wide detour of the pool to avoid a repetition of the earlier experience. The pool no longer exists which is a pity for the present generation, for we used to have a lovely time sliding on the ice during the winter, in our every-day shoes. Skates were unknown to us. I seem to remember it being much colder in those days during the winter, and much hotter in the summer.

We, as children, were not aware of it at the time, but Professor Thomas Merton financed the Christmas parties in the Parish Hall for the children of the village, and each and everyone of us received a present out of the bran tub, selected by dipping our hands into the tub. As well as being a brilliant scientist and inventor, Professor Merton was an extremely kind and generous person. He owned the fishing rights on the river Wye and any member of the village community had permission to fish without a licence. His footman, Mr Morris, was instructed to buy school books for the boys and girls.

Charley Donald was the gamekeeper on the professor's estate at Winforton House and lived at Chestnut Cottage, which belonged to the estate. It was once two semi-detached cottages with a tailor living in one end and a cobbler in the other. Charley was responsible for rounding up the beaters for the professor's shoot, to which he had invited all his friends, and as we were practically neighbours and willing to please, we were among the first to be collared and invited to collaborate. This involved rising earlier than the pheasants and throwing a ring round the wood or coppice to make sure that the birds did not escape; keeping them inside for the gentry's satisfaction of at least having a shot at them. Fortunately, a lot of them survived to tell the tale—today it is my opinion that pheasants are too beautiful to kill—but our job then was first to prevent them flying out of the wood. Eventually the professor and his guests would arrive after we had been waiting for three or four hours. They would position themselves at intervals round the wood, taking good care they would not be shooting one another, and my father and I, together with members of the village, would enter the wood and begin to beat whatever was in sight, such as trees and bushes, so that the birds would fly out into the path of the guns. For this, as boys we were paid half-a-crown (12.5p), and the men 5/- (25p). This was for a day's work starting at 5 a.m. and finishing at lunch time to which I had looked forward with immense relish, because we were given beef and mustard sandwiches with lots of lovely hot sweet tea—don't forget this was in the midst of winter and we were very cold. Whilst it was Charley Donald's job to see that everyone was paid, lunch took place at Winforton House in the stables under the supervision of Percy, the butler.

Jim and Sid Davies, the latter of whom is the only surviving member of the community of that era still living in Winforton at the time of writing, told me that when they were rabbiting in the area— we were all talented naturalists in those days—if Donald, the gamekeeper, arrived or was seen in the distance, they would whip the nets off the rabbit burrows, leaving the ferrets, and would jump over the hedge into Wood Farm. If they met Charley he would inquire as to where they had been. 'Oh,' they'd say, 'just out for a walk and looking for our ferrets.' 'Are these the ones?' Charley would ask and they would say, 'Oh, they must have strayed a good way from home.'

One day Jim Davies was walking across one of Roger Powell's fields belonging to Winforton Court, and Roger happened to see him and called out: 'Where are you going my boy?' — he thought he was going rabbiting on his land—'come 'ere I want to show you summat.' Mr Powell took Jim up into a special room at the top of his house where there were some stocks that had been there for centuries, sometimes used to imprison marauders from over the border in Wales and said, 'If I do see you poachin' rabbits on my land in future, I'll put you in them there stocks, understand?'

Jim was only ten years old and trembling in his boots said, 'Yes Sir, Mr Powell I do understand what you mean, but I was only going fishin' in the river,' and Jim proceeded to the river, but he never crossed Powell's field again. (The infamous Hanging Judge, Baron Jeffries of Wem, held court at Winforton Court where there was a windowless cell, a whipping post which has since been removed to make room for a billiards table, and some stocks in the attic where prisoners were detained until they were brought to trial.)

In those days there were far more rabbits about than even during the 1950s when myxomatosis was introduced into the country by one of the rabbits that had got away from the French professor who had been injecting them with a substance that caused the disease, climbed aboard one of the ferries from St Malo in Brittany, and had disembarked in Portsmouth to infest the rabbits in this country! Rabbits were a great asset during the 1920s and provided a cheap protein which was as nutritious as more expensive meat such as beef and pork. Catching rabbits with ferrets and nets was a most enjoyable pastime for us boys as well as profitable, because even round the village they could be sold for 6d each. We used snares as well as gin traps. We put the snares on the rabbit runs and the traps at the entrance to the burrows and covered them with dried grass to camouflage them, and went round in the mornings to collect the catch. Not many people could afford a shotgun except the toffs, but there were many ways of obtaining an inexpensive meal. The following verse was very popular at the time:-

For rabbits young and rabbits old
For rabbits hot and rabbits cold
For rabbits tender, rabbits tough
We thank the Lord we've had enough

I remember rabbiting once with my cousin John Jay, who was a few years older than myself, within hearing distance of the family's farmhouse. I became wildly excited when several rabbits bolted out into the nets to the point that I uttered such expletives that poor old John was in fear of me being heard by his mother and father who forbade such behaviour.

Mum and Dad never went to market without loading up the trap with rabbits, which were easily sold around Hay in the hotels and private residences—I don't think Major Armstrong, the Hay murderer, was one of their customers—if not in the market because other people had the same idea. We could always go knocking on doors even if we had to reduce the price. If we used the rabbits ourselves we could sell the skins for 2d to Augustus Edwards of the Tannery in Hereford, which was our source for disposing of other skins such as those of squirrels and weasels accidentally caught in gin-traps, and fox skins, from foxes which had been caught in a vicious fox trap or sometimes in the gin-traps if they were properly pegged down. Squirrels', weasels' and stoats' skins we sold for 2d each and fox skins for 6d.

Mole skins were another source of revenue which were sold for 1d. We caught them in proper mole traps. One fellow in the village had a mole making a tremendous mess of his newly-laid lawn. He said 'I'll catch the bugger; I'm going to buy a double barrelled shotgun and some cartridges. I'll blow the blighter to smithereens,' and sat on the back door step to wait for the mole to put in an appearance! He's probably still there!

The poultry, that is ducks, geese, chickens and turkeys, were killed and dressed all the year round, but especially at Christmas. When we were old enough, from five onwards, we would all be expected to have a go at plucking feathers, looking very much like poultry ourselves when we were covered with feathers, ready for

9

mother to do the dressing. Aunt Alice, if Uncle Bert could manage without her for the day, used to drive down from Prospect Farm, Clifford, with the pony and float bringing with her John and Edwin, the latter of whom was still a babe in arms and in the pram, to give mother a hand with the feathering and dressing. (Tommy, the pony, was quite a character and always looked as though he was trotting sideways. He lived to a great age for a horse, to over 30, and worked right up to the day he dropped dead. I suppose that's the best way for anybody to go.) Chickens were sold for about 4 or 5/- (20 to 25p) and turkeys for around 9/-. If we couldn't sell them in Hay Market, we'd again have to go knocking on doors. It was essential that we dispose of them as we couldn't take them home—there was no deep freeze or ice-box. Some people used to hold their own auctions in the market after it had closed; there were always people hanging around waiting for something cheap, or better still *gratis*; there were a lot of hungry people about with two million unemployed. They did not get Social Security as today, only Parish Relief and they were lucky if they got 5/- a week for a family of six.

Because there was no railway station in Winforton, or stock lorries on the road, Dad had to drive any animals he had for sale along the road to Hay Market across the toll bridge at Whitney-on-Wye and pay a charge of 1d per animal, and if they were not sold he would have to take them home to return the following week. The toll had to be paid both ways and it was no good telling Mr John Taylor, the collector, that they were the same animals you had had to pay for on the way to market—you only had to pay for yourself one way if you were driving animals. If you were riding a bike you had to pay 1d for the bike and 1d for yourself.

Because the roads were so rough—J. L. McAdam had died in 1836 and had forgotten the tar—people had to shoe their geese before driving them to market with a tar substance. They either dipped the goose's foot into a bucket of the stuff, or painted it on to protect their feet from any bruising. There is a street in Carmarthen called 'Heol-y-gwyddau'—the Road of the Geese. It was obviously the street through which the farmers drove their geese to market.

Some people had a pig-sty in their back garden as well as a chicken run, the pig-sty in one corner and the chicken run in the other. But with us having a bit of ground, a few acres, we had several sows rooting about. Even though they were rung—had rings in their noses—they'd still turn up the ground with their snouts. During the autumn they would have a wonderful time acorning; you'd hardly have to feed them with anything, there would be so many acorns about. Outdoor pigs, I understand, never get anaemia. The piglets would run with their mothers, but you'd have to make sure they were safely tucked up in bed at night otherwise the foxes might have them!

Mr Whitefoot was the acknowledged official pig-killer in our area which paid him 2/6d for slaughtering a pig and cutting it up next day. The 'moon had to be right' before a pig was killed, and to be sure of this Old Moor's Almanac had to be consulted so that the bacon was cured properly. We required some strong men, depending on the size of the animal which itself depended on the size of the family, but we usually killed at 15 score, 300 lbs, and this after a sow had had several litters. The pig had to be handled with extreme gentleness, as if it bruised the bacon couldn't be cured properly. The first part of the operation, nauseating in retrospect, was to place a whipcord round the pig's upper jaw. This would be done in the sty and then the pig would be helped along to the bench where the dastardly act was to be performed, by tickling up its rear or holding a bucket of feed under its nose to encourage it along the way. Once it had arrived Mr Whitefoot would grab its ears and lower jaw, one of the men would grasp its right front leg and double it up underneath, whilst one of the others would clutch a rear leg. With the assistance of another helper everybody, on Mr Whitefoot's command, would swiftly lift the animal onto a low bench and Mr Whitefoot would rapidly stick the pig at the same time, severing the main artery to the heart (sticking is a delicate operation which involves cutting the main blood vessels in order to bleed the carcass as quickly and as completely as possible). All this time the poor old pig would be squealing its and everybody's head off, but sometimes to reduce the commotion the cord that had been placed around the upper jaw would be wound round the pig's mouth. This operation had to be carried out with speed and precision. To hold the animal down on the bench the men would lean on it with all their weight, including all of my father's 7 stones! (Once, when staying at Pen-tri-coed on my uncle's farm, a pig of 20 score which was being slaughtered didn't approve of what the pig-killer was doing to it, and managed to get off the bench after it had been stuck and ran around the farmyard until it eventually collapsed through loss of blood). The pig would have been laid on its side so that the blood would drain into a clean enamel bowl or bucket, as the blood was used to make black-pudding—Yorkshire is not its only home.

When the pig had expired and the blood had been totally drained, the animal was lowered onto the ground on all fours, and straw placed on and around it and set on fire to burn off the bristles, being careful not to disfigure the carcass. Once this was achieved, scalding hot water would be required to harden the skin so that it could be scraped clean. When this was accomplished the carcass would be hung indoors, usually in the larder, or if no larder, the kitchen where the butcher would slit the pig's belly down the middle and remove the entrails. This part of the operation had to be carried out within at least 24 hours as offal can quickly deteriorate. There's a lot of awful offal, but also edible offal such as lungs, heart, kidneys and pancreas, some of which was always distributed among the helpers as an incentive for their co-operation. In any event it had to be disposed of quickly in one way or another as there was no means of preserving the meat, so the best thing was for everybody to have a jolly good fry-up for supper, probably about the only time we could invite the neighbours for a meal.

The following morning Mr Whitefoot would return to complete his task and proceed to first remove the head from which Mother used to make brawn, then the trotters and hocks, followed by the hams and shoulders which would be laid onto a salting stone that had already been covered with a thick layer of salt, then the sides of the pig which when they had been cured would be called flitches. We then covered the whole with another layer of salt, making sure that it was packed well down between the cuts and round the edges. Sometimes the gammons were salted separately. Saltpetre would be inserted into the hole from where the knuckle and socket had been removed. The bacon would remain salted for several weeks. Meanwhile the heart, lungs, gullet, spleen and tongue were usually minced to make faggots and sausages. A lot of this would be sold to the villagers at giveaway prices. The bladder was washed and dried and could be used as a container for lard, when not being used as a football! The large and small intestines, as well as the stomach, were used as containers for sausages and puddings of various kinds. When the meat had been cured, it was well washed to remove all surplus salt and then dried and hung on hooks from the ceiling in the larder or kitchen, but sometimes we would first rub brown sugar or honey into the bacon to improve the taste, or stick it up the chimney to smoke it. We would then, at not too far some distant date, slice rashers off as required, or cut a chunk off and boil it. Bacon was one of the least expensive meats; beef was too expensive at 6d per pound, even for brisket, the cheapest cut.

The few fields of Nicholas Farm unfortunately were not lumped together, but were scattered about in all directions. My parents did most of the work even during the harvesting of hay and corn. We had one lovely field of ten acres in front of the house on which we sometimes planted wheat, barley or oats, and my Father, who was a dab hand with a scythe, would soon, as he would say, make short work of it; for his size he was as strong as a horse and like lightning in anything he undertook. My Mother would follow behind bundling the corn into sheaves, each sheaf being bound with several strands of straw and then placed into stooks, eight to ten sheaves forming a stook, and then left for a week to ten days in the field for the corn to dry, or longer if it rained. The less it was handled the better. When it was dry it would be hauled into the barn and stacked ready for threshing when it could be thrown down into the passage between the doors onto canvas sheets and threshed by my parents with flails. The straw would then be stacked on the other side of the barn until it was needed. The threshed corn was then winnowed by throwing it up into the air from a special basket, for the wind to blow away the chaff and leave the heavier gain to fall back onto the sheet. Oat and barley straw was fed to the cattle in the winter, whilst the wheat straw went into the yards to be trodden and dunged on.

Grass was cut the same way as corn with a scythe and it was turned several times with a wooden rake before it was dry enough to be pushed into tumps or hay cocks and then loaded onto a sledge or gamble, a gamble being a flat wooden bed with two wheels and two shafts and drawn by a horse. Dad did the pitching with a pitch-fork and mother was up on the gamble loading the hay in such a way to prevent it slipping. When I was old enough, about seven or eight, I was allowed to lead the horse from one cock to the other and would have to shout 'Hold fast' or 'Hold tight' — this to my mother mind you before moving off to the next tump. I thought I was doing a very important job and was a big man. You'll never forget the smell of new mown hay or the sound of a horse-drawn mowing machine, though this was to come later on when I became a farm student on an uncle's farm near Ledbury, Herefordshire. My Father was never in a position to own such a mowing machine. Farming conditions were harsh and very difficult in the 1920s caused by a complete neglect of home agriculture and a flooding of the country with cheap imports from all over the world. By 1930 they had worsened to such a degree that prices fell to below what it cost to produce. The main thing for most farmers was to raise sufficient cash to pay the rent, as almost all farms and smallholdings were rented for approximately £1 an acre. There were three million unemployed in 1932 and farming was in the depths of depression. A cow that was worth £70 in 1920 was worth only £15 in 1930, and all possessions had depreciated in the same way. Many farmers packed it in and tried to seek work elsewhere, which was like jumping out of the frying pan into the fire as there were so many unemployed already.

Whilst most farmers rented their farms, my parents owned theirs. It had been left to them by my grandfather, George Jay, who died when I was only one year old, aged 86. It's unsurprising that I don't remember my grandfather, though I have a photograph of him. From what I understand he was a 'gentleman farmer' always dressed up to the nines. He also liked his pint of beer. Dad said he worked his little wife, Elizabeth, to the bone, in which there may be some truth, because Grandmother Jay died two years before him in 1919 aged 68.

Against my Father's better judgment he was persuaded to sell Nicholas Farm by a certain gentleman who had bought Little Wood Farm at Upper Pitch, Winforton, and who offered it to Dad on a rental basis. I think because of the depression the rot had set in by then, and Father was on his way down the slippery slope. Soon after we moved one of the cows broke out and wandered off into a nearby wood and gorged itself to death on rhododendron leaves, not knowing any the better, which were said to have poisoned her. This was a terrible loss in what was already the worst economic recession of their lives. I remember too that Mother returned from Hay Market with two lovely white doves, and no sooner had they been let out of their dovecot then they took flight never to return. They say that life is full of disappointments, but some have more than others.

Horses were my Father's delight. When he was in his 80s I took him to London for the day one Sunday. When I asked him if he'd like to go he said 'Yes, as long as we can go to church when we get there.'

'Don't worry', I replied, 'we'll get there in time.' We arrived just in time for the morning's service at the Bloomsbury Baptist Church. When the service ended and we returned to the car we hadn't gone many yards before we met two Metropolitan Mounted Police which prompted Dad to tell me to stop the car as he wanted to walk back the way we had just come so that he could have a good look at the two magnificent black police horses. He loved horses of all kinds and spent a considerable part of his life breaking them in, both what we used to call cart-horses, or what some people call shire horses, and horses for riding—which he preferred of course. He should have been a jockey because he was of the right size, but it would have involved gambling and he was dead against that sort of thing. He was well known in the area as having a way with horses and people brought them for him to school. Some people are very brutal in the way they break a horse, but my father was kind and gentle. They'd almost do exactly as he wanted them to do just by talking to them gently.

My Father used to put the foals into a stall as soon as they had been taken from their mother, put a halter on and tie them up so that they became used to their environment. When about six month's old they were docked; that is they had their tales cut off. Later, at about 12 months they were castrated and this had to be done before they were broken in for work. It wasn't very often that a horse or mare was broken in until it was three year's old unless it was on a small-holding on which they could not afford to keep a horse that long before putting it to work. Horses were generally broken in in the Autumn. For days or a week beforehand they used to put some tackle on them with some mouthing equipment—a bit through the mouth which had three little chains on it so as to soften the mouth to make it easier to handle. It also had what they call a surcingle, such an a stallion has round its middle and over its back with a crupper under its tail, buckled to the back of the saddle, with the mouthing tackle connected to the surcingle, so that it will hold its head up, at the same time hardening its jaws.

Soon after, they would get the horse on a halter and out into a field where the ground was soft in case the animal threw itself down in a fit of temper and where it wouldn't hurt itself. Very often the trainers would drive an iron bar into the ground and put a rope with a noose on it and trot the horse round one way before making it go the opposite way. Then they would get some jo-tackle and gears that they used for ploughing, putting a collar and harness on the horse, with jo-tackle over its back with the traces. With all this gear they would trot the horse round so as to make as much noise an possible with the equipment, getting it used to the noise. Afterwards they'd make the horse pull a log behind it to get it used to pulling something. Very often the horse was put into some gears that were called long-gears, such as chains, between two working horses. It was usual to start them to work in that way, Some farmers would have a shafter or a six ring furrow press, some of which were almost immovable; they were like fixtures and terrible things to turn. (They should have been outlawed). Later they were improved and the contraption became more mobile on a spindle which made it much easier for the horse to operate. I suspect that the former was an extremely brutal way of breaking in a horse.

One has to be more careful with riding horses and a little more gentle, especially if they are thoroughbreds, as they are more sensitive. First one has to put a dummy on their backs after the preliminaries in the same way as breaking in a shire horse. The dummy is a sort of sack stuffed with straw which is tied onto the part of the mane on top of the crop. They didn't put a saddle onto the horse until it got used to the sack at which time they took it for a long walk or put it on a good long lunging rein as it is called today or a leading rein attached to the bit. When the horse had got used to the dummy, someone, usually joe-soap, would have to get up onto the horse's back and into the saddle with someone else leading the horse round the field by the bridle, until it had quietened down and, hopefully, been broken in.

Actually, Dad never used a dummy for breaking in a horse. He always spent a lot of time and patience leaning on a horse's back before mounting it; he also used to drive it round the meadow on some joe lines so that it would get used to the feel of something on its sides, and when he mounted the horse he would keep his legs still and straight without touching its belly even before putting a saddle on it. Eventually he'd put the saddle on the horse and walk it round and round the field, first one way and then the other until it got used to the dangling stirrups. A horse, in the early stages, will go up the wall and round the bend if it feels anything touching its sides. I don't think that my Father ever found a horse to be unbreakable or impossible to school. There is some very good advice chipped out of a drinking trough in what is now Llandeilo's car park which says: 'The Merciful man is merciful to his beast'. I am sure my Father would have agreed.

Approaching school leaving age at 14 and as, unlike my sister, Mary, I did not pass my 11 plus, it was arranged that I should pursue and extend my agricultural career with my uncle and aunt, Leonard and Emily Price, at their farm at Veldt House, Ledbury, where they had a herd of pedigree Friesian cows producing Grade A Tuberculin Tested milk. So, on reaching the age of 14, I left Winforton to start work for my uncle and aunt.

2
To be a Farmer's Boy

Uncle Leonard, who was married to my father's sister Emily, was in 1934 considered to be a prosperous farmer compared with many in the country. He had done well in the First World War, and even though at the end of the war he hadn't lived a life of partying, playing tennis and golf with no thought for tomorrow, as had many, he had a rude awakening when the depression fell upon him in the late 1920s. One of the ways to prosper during this period was to be a dairy farmer, and Uncle Leonard had a pedigree Friesian dairy herd of about 30 cows, plus a bull, and although he could have managed without a trouble-maker like myself, he and Aunt Emily, more so to help my parents, took me on as an assistant to the cowman. Bill Symonds instantly hated my guts; the first thing he did was to give me a piece of chewing tobacco that made me feel that the cowshed was going round and round. From that very moment I used to keep out of his way as far as it was humanly possible, which turned out to be very difficult in the restricted confines of a cowshed.

It was understood that I should go to the Veldt House to further my education in the farming world for 6/- (30p) a week, plus board and lodging. I was to be available seven days a week come hail, rain or shine, for whatever was required of me, but would be treated as one of the family and expected to go to church with my uncle and aunt. There was no dodging the issue. The Veldt House was a beautiful Elizabethan timber-framed, black and white house with electric light and all mod cons, and Aunt Emily was a wonderful housekeeper. Everything was spick and span, and every time you went into the house you had to take your boots off and put your slippers on, and make sure you washed your face and hands before you set foot in the kitchen. There was an outside toilet in which there was a roll of blue toilet paper!

Being principally a dairy farm it was essential to make an early start, and it came as somewhat of a shock to the system to discover that one had to rise at 6 a.m. all the year round, and to sally forth regardless of the elements towards the cowshed without even a cup of tea to warm the cockles of your heart—today I wouldn't budge an inch without my cuppa. The first thing we had to do, or should I say *I* had to do, because of course it was left 'to the boy', was to muck out. It was January when I started and mid-winter, and as such the cows remained indoors and fouled their sleeping quarters, consequently it had to be cleaned out before the main operation of milking began. The next thing was to wash their udders and clean their flanks—cows are not as clean as pigs—and this had to be done with warm water and wiped again before sitting down to milk each cow. We sat on a three-legged stool and held a milk pail firmly between our knees. Unless a cow was a first time calver she would stand still to be milked, as she would be used to it, but on rare occasions it might be necessary to tie a cow's hind legs about the hocks to prevent either leg being used to kick the milker. A cow only kicks if she is being hurt or is frightened, and usually that's because she has been brutalised, but once the habit has been formed it is difficult to break. It is much better to be patient and gentle with a cow as with any other animal, in which case you'll achieve your objective. Cows are creatures of habit. Once you've decided which two teats to pull, you start milking. In reality you don't just pull but gently squeeze, otherwise the cow would kick you out through the door onto the muck heap. We were supposed to wear white coats and hats as the Milk Marketing Board was very particular about cleanliness. After all, the milk was Grade A Tuberculin Tested and somewhat special.

It would take us a couple of hours to milk the cows, taking each bucket of milk round to the dairy and pouring the milk into a container on a stand, so that it would run down the cooler into a ten gallon churn, before returning once again to the grind. I can never remember any of the cows suffering from mastitis, the reason for this being that the cows were milked by hand and we took every precaution to prevent bacterial infection which causes inflammation of the udder. The udders were thoroughly washed and dried and all dirt removed.

When we had finished milking, the cows were turned out for the day to forage for themselves, and when they were brought in for the evening's milking they were fed concentrates to keep them quiet whilst being milked, and hay and roots afterwards; roots being mangolds or swedes which yours truly had to cut up with a machine.

Before breakfast we had to wash the milking utensils with hot water and thoroughly sterilise everything used for milk. I say we, but again I did most of the work as the cowman had already gone home for his breakfast. After we'd had a meal uncle would get out the car and trailer and take the churns of milk down to the milk stand at the bottom of the drive ready for the Milk Marketing lorry to pick up. The M.M.B. had been formed in 1933 and paid 8d a gallon in the summer and 10d a gallon in the winter. Uncle's cows were a pedigree herd and the yield was generally high, in the region of 2,000 gallons, but he had one cow that yielded a record 2,750 gallons; she won first prize at the Reading cattle show and her calves were greatly valued needless to say. Most of the heifer calves would be retained to replenish the existing herd, but the bull calves, once they had put on a few pounds, would go the way of all bull calves in due course. When the cows were brought in at roughly 5 p.m. for the evening milking, the process was repeated, but the milk churns were left in the dairy until the following morning. In those days we lived in a more law-abiding country than today, but even so it was not advisable to leave 50 or 60 gallons of milk by the road overnight. Someone might have developed a thirst!

Being the boy on the farm there were a number of jobs I could do without much supervision, and spent many a lonely hour all by myself doing just that; one was stone picking in the fields whereby you were required to take a swath of about four yards at a time and put the stones in little heaps, using a bucket in which to collect them. This was not an entirely constructive job of work, but at least you were helping to prevent future accidents with the mowing machine. A heavy roller would be used afterwards, in part to make sure that any stones you had missed were safely pushed into the ground. Later, the wagoner, or some would call him the carter, Jack Colwall, would arrive with a horse and cart to remove the stones which would usually be taken to fill in gateways which had become knee deep in mud through constant use by the animals.

One of the jobs I hated most was creosoting wooden fences because I used to get it all over myself, and it stung like the blazes and was difficult to get off without loads of soap and hot water. I would spend all morning or afternoon being burned up with the horrible stuff, because there was no going home for cups of tea as an excuse to clean up. You had to keep at it, as they say, and suffer in silence.

During the time I was at the Veldt House uncle had a windfall, he discovered that two of his fields produced 10cwt. of mushrooms, with some encouragement from sheep. The two fields, totalling 8 acres, were called 'near bargains' and 'far bargains'. Mushrooms have to be picked quickly otherwise they soon go off, and although Leonora and Dorothy, uncle's two daughters were away from home, Leonora as a nurse and Dorothy at a boarding school, they always seemed to appear for the mushroom harvest. I never knew whether uncle had some secret arrangement with the hospital and school, or that it just happened that their holidays fell at a very propitious time, as they always turned up when required. Picking mushrooms of that quantity involves early rising and we were out cutting—you don't pick them otherwise you pull them out at the root and destroy the spawn—by the car's head-lamps at 3 o'clock in the morning, including Uncle Leonard. We picked them in 3 lb flimsey wooden chip baskets and placed them in the trailer hitched to the Wolsey 14. After being weighed they were taken to Ledbury Station to be sent to Leeds where uncle had secured a contract for the season at 3d per lb. There was an unlimited supply of mushrooms and quite a lot were wasted as it was impossible to get round them all; naturally while they lasted we were never short of mushrooms to go with our bacon for breakfast, and they were delicious as only wild mushrooms can be. But the milking had to be done first, so that when we had finished gathering the fungus it was to the cowshed to help Bill. He invariably would ask, 'Where 'ave you bin then? 'ave you bin gettin' up late or summat?'

There's one incident I shall never forget. Uncle had four horses, carthorses or shires; two mares and two geldings, and one spring some nine days after one of the mares had foaled we had a visit from the local stallion that was on one of his circuits—stallions were walked around on circuits, not driven around in lorries, and worked an area that included hundreds of mares. Stallions were a sight to behold, done up to the nines with their bobbed, ribboned tails and tasselled mane, horse brasses, surcingle and bridle; they looked a picture enough to drive any mare loco. When this stallion turned into the drive off the main road, he knew he was in for a good time, and started neighing to let the mare know he was on his way and it wouldn't be long now.

You should have a trying bar to keep the horses apart until you are sure the mare is properly in season, but uncle only had a gate to put between them which was used as the teasing bar. Jack Colwall would be pretty sure that the mare was ready and the handler, the groom, would know fairly quickly if the mare responded to the stallion's love making. He teased the mare by playfully biting her neck, just like a human being, or rubbing his head against hers. If the mare was not ready she would start lashing out at the gate between them, but a good groom would not allow the situation to reach that stage. If the mare was not very interested the stallion is left to tease the mare to bring her on, and once she is ready and receptive they would open the gate and put them together. The groom and the wagoner would have to be quite sure that the mare was ready, because a stallion worth a few hundred pounds could easily get hurt.

A stallion needs assistance as he can't manage by himself, but that's left to the reader's imagination because I'm not going into details. After spending so much time with the foreplay it is over in a flash and on this occasion the mare conceived; there was no need for a return journey. If she hadn't it would have meant making another attempt in three weeks time. Sometimes it is very difficult to get a mare to foal because they slip and it might mean having to return umpteen times before being successful. By the time the mare had foaled, I had left the scene for greener pastures, but I understand that she had a lovely little brown filly with white socks and blaze on its forehead.

One of the fiddling jobs I hated was clipping the edges of the lawn with sheep shearing shears, along the paths and round the flower beds, and worst of all weeding the paths with a knife. Of course, boys always think they are more mature than they are and should be doing something of importance.

Every year they had an annual sports day at Much Marcle. I had been allowed to take the afternoon off the first year I was at the Veldt and had admired very much the long distance runners taking part in the three mile race. Thinking that the following year I might be able to take part I began training, and whenever possible would run several times round one of the fields, but it was a waste of time and energy as nobody recognised my talent (!) and I hadn't the courage to suggest that I might take part in the races.

As has previously been mentioned my uncle and aunt were staunch church goers, and every Sunday morning we would go to either the Quaker Church in Ross-on-Wye, the Quakers' in Worcester, or the Methodists' in Ledbury. I preferred the latter because it was much the same as I had been used to, with hymns, prayers and a sermon, but with the Quakers you just sat still for an hour precisely until the Spirit 'moved' somebody. There was no music or singing which for me was the essence of a church service. What does a boy of 14 or 15 think about if he's just sitting still? Probably looking at some pretty girl and wishing he could go for long walks in the country with her, but certainly not communing with one's soul which is what you were supposed to do. Nevertheless, I shall always be grateful for the Christian background provided by my parents, because although in later life I somewhat strayed from the straight and narrow, there have been many times when it has been necessary for me to get down on my hands and knees. If you haven't had a Christian home life during your formative years, I would imagine that it is difficult to know where to turn during times of trouble. I am thankful to my parents; my only regret is not having shown more appreciation whilst they were alive. We have to suffer from our thoughtlessness in later life.

One day Aunt Emily gave me the news that they were going to set me up in business, giving me two sheep, for which I was most grateful. If I had stuck it out they would have grown into quite a flock I'm sure, but being born like a troubled sea I was not to witness the growth of my flock. It never even occurred to me at the time that there would ever be more than just two sheep. I did not envisage the possibility of the two sheep growing into a flock of 100, with lots of baaing lambs following their bleating mothers, which was rather short-sighted of me.

But life took a sudden turn, caused by an advertisement in the *Hereford Times* during 1936 of Sainsbury's wanting boys to train as assistants in their grocery and butchery departments in Tottenham, London. I suggested to my aunt that I would like to go for an interview which was to take place in Worcester. How I ever plucked up the courage to do that, goodness knows. I was never capable of stringing two words together to voice an opinion of any kind let alone argue about something, unless I had been sulking as people do who are not capable of expressing themselves. There was no discussion whatsoever about why or wherefore, and my aunt kindly arranged for me to be taken to the interview. Two weeks later, after being reckoned to be of sound mind and body and just before my 16th birthday, I left on my first train journey from Great Malvern to Paddington one bright and frosty morning without even visiting my parents to bid them farewell. Youth can be a thoughtless, inconsiderate age. As for my sheep, Aunt Emily sent me their value of £5, which was a lot of money and should have lasted a long time, with it costing only 6d to go to the pictures.

3
To be a Butcher's Boy

So on Saturday, 18 January 1936, I arrived in the Big Smoke for the first time in my life, eight days before my 16th birthday, with the sheep money of £5 in my pocket and a job to go to—which is more than a lot of youngsters have today when they arrive in London. Of course, my first priority was to find my way to Tottenham which for a yobbo fresh from the green fields of Herefordshire was not an easy matter. Even today when I find myself in the Underground maze, I'm never quite sure where I'm going to end up and always have to ask someone the way. However, after a few false starts I eventually found my way to the rooms where those starting with Sainsbury's were provided with board and lodgings. We were exceedingly well provided for as we lived above a butchery and grocery store, where we lacked for nothing in the way of provisions! Our pay was the princely sum of 10/- (50p) a week.

Bernard Jay Wallis, though I never believed that was his name, was our spiritual guide and mentor. From the first moment he never had any time for us and always had 'to go and see a man about a dog'. He might have been keen on greyhounds for which there are many race tracks in the London area, as I know to my cost, but I suspect his interest lay in another direction as he was very good looking and wasn't short of a friend or two of the opposite sex. After being allotted our beds and shown the dining room we retired and prepared for the following morning. We were to report for work at 7.45 a.m. in time for a 'neck and finger-nail' inspection by B.J.W. He lined us up that day and for many more with our hands stretched out with palms faced downwards, so that he could see that our nails were clean, and then he'd walk round the back to inspect our necks! There were four of us; two for the butcher's shop and two for the grocery store. Then we would proceed to our respective posts and begin the day's scrubbing and cleaning of the premises—'you don't think you are going to handle a butcher's knife do you? You'll cut yourself'—which were enormous. So much for being a butcher's trainee, but that's the way of all apprenticeships is it not?

After many times of cleaning out every nook and cranny, both on the floors and ceilings; cleaning and polishing all the windows— no outside window cleaners were then employed—washing and scrubbing every conceivable service and sterilising all the tools of the trade, B.J.W. said we might be entrusted to handle some of the knives, especially the 8 inch radial-pointed, flat, flexible, curved blade knife essential for boning. But first it was suggested that before using any knife it should be sharpened on a 12 inch steel, first one side and then the other, 'making sure you don't take the skin of the knuckle of your first finger!'

The four principally utilised tools of a butcher were a boning knife, a hack-saw, a cleaver and, of course, a steel. We were always advised to use a hack-saw to cut a bone instead of the cleaver, because the latter sometimes splintered the bones making a terrible mess, as well as resulting in having to pick up every splinter for miles around.

We were allowed to go out at night, and occasionally I made for the Odeon Cinema at Edmonton, up Tottenham Road, which was only ten minutes away. The rest of the time I'd familiarise myself with the district and gradually ventured further afield. Life continued in a hum-drum sort of way as there was not much one could do on 10/- a week, other than go to the pictures and walk about sight-seeing during one's leisure hours. Travelling by tram in those days enabled one to see the noteworthy features of the city and, one Sunday afternoon, I found myself in the West End, not having been there before. Walking up from Piccadilly Circus towards Hyde Park Corner I was greeted by a lady of mature years, between 30 and 40 at least, as though we had met before, who said she was French and would I like to spend some time with her. I was somewhat taken aback as I couldn't think what it was she wanted of me, so I said, 'But I don't know you.'

'Oh' she said, 'that's no problem, we'll soon get to know one another,' and she began to take hold of my hand and pull me along the street.

I asked her where she was taking me and she said 'To my flat, of course.'

'Oh,' I said, 'I can't go there' and stood my ground.

'No?' she said. 'If I like you, you can be my boyfriend and I'll look after you.'

I replied that I didn't want a girlfriend as I was only just 16 and a long way from home, and would she please excuse me as I had to return to my place of employment, and that we might be able to make arrangements for another day. She let me go, much to my relief. I was really scared out of my mind. Goodness knows what she had on hers, though I had a vague idea.

Having escaped the clutches of the dragon—I can still see her 55 years on—I carried on along Piccadilly and made my way round towards Victoria Station, but instead of going to the station I turned left up Buckingham Gate which proved absolutely fatal. This, by the way was at a brisk pace so as to put as much space between myself and the French lady, so that I did not entirely know where I was going, but it turned out that I was on my way to Buckingham Palace and who should I see outside guarding the King, but the Grenadier Guards resplendent in bearskin and red tunic. My foreseeable future was at once decided though I had to make some inquiries as to the possibility of my being able to march up and down outside Buckingham Palace (the grass has always been greener on the other side of the hill for me you see, and they say a rolling stone gathers no moss, which is why after all these years I am still skint). So I had the brilliant idea of going up to one of the sentries and asked him how I could become a guardsman to which he replied, muttering under his breath, something like 'me no speaky, ask a policeman you twit'.

Of course, I did not realise it at the time, a sentry is not supposed to speak to the public, let alone look to his left or right or turn his head. So as there were always a number of metropolitan police in the area I approached one of them. He suggested that there was probably a recruiting office in Tottenham, but that I'd have to be 18 before I could join the army. I replied that I didn't want to join the army, but the Grenadier Guards wearing bearskins and red tunics.

'Never mind' the policeman said, 'the recruiting sergeant will tell you all about it when you see him.' He paused. 'When are you going to the recruiting office?'

'Oh', I said 'I shall not be able to go until my half day off next Thursday afternoon.'

'Do you think you'll be able to wait that long?' the policeman inquired. Then he wanted to know how old I was, and I told him I was just 16 years of age.

'Oh,' he said, 'you're not old enough, so you'll have to put your age on a couple of years like I did, only I was 17 when I joined the Welsh Guards. Why don't you join the Welsh Guards?'

'I'm not Welsh I'm an Englishman' I said. 'Where do the Grenadiers come from?' The policeman said it was an English regiment, but all sorts of people join it.. 'Well, I'm going to join it because I was born in England,' and left Constable Williams with my head held high, feeling like 18 years of age and already marching like a guardsman. I followed the policeman's instructions, crossing Constitution Hill and returning to Piccadilly through Green Park, hoping that I would not come face to face with the French prostitute. As I approached Piccadilly and made for the Underground, I walked on the opposite side of the street and quickened my pace, not looking to left or right just in case I should glimpse her out of the corner of my eye, or that she should glimpse me. I bounded down those steps three at a time and sailed through the enfolding doors of the awaiting train just in time, and with a sigh of relief.

My Sunday afternoon's jaunt put me off my stride and until the following Thursday afternoon, when I intended visiting the Recruiting Office up the road, I spent my waking hours mooning about, contemplating what I was going to say to the recruiting sergeant, and wondering how I could make myself look two years older. I didn't think that two days growth on my upper lip would make a lot of difference as I had only just begun to shave. At night I spent my time dreaming that I was on guard outside Buckingham Palace, and that all the tourists came to look at me and my red tunic and bearskin.

Finally, the big day came and without a whisper to anyone, having given the Recruiting Sergeant time to recover from his lunch hour, I entered his office trying not to make too much noise and with some hesitation.

'Don't be afraid my boy, what can I do for you?' the sergeant said.

I told him of my experience the previous Sunday afternoon, and that I had been attracted by the uniform of the sentries on guard at Buckingham Palace, explaining that I would like to march up and down outside the Palace to guard the King. He replied that it was not quite as simple as that, that there would be a long, arduous training and preparation and asked me which regiment I wanted to join. I said the Grenadier Guards. The recruiting sergeant, who was a Grenadier himself, said that there were other regiments, but agreed that as I was an Englishman I should join the Grenadiers. He then needed to know how old I was and my height. I replied that I was just 18 in January, and that my height was 5'10" which in those days was the minimum height—I believe today they enlist men above 5'8"—the sergeant seemed satisfied so far, but inquired as to whether I really wanted to join the army.

I said, 'I'm not having to join the army, am I?' To perform ceremonial duties such as guarding His Majesty the King I thought they were some sort of toy soldiers. The sergeant said they'll give you toy soldiers when they're chasing your bollocks off around that parade ground. I replied that I didn't care what they did to me as long as I could wear a red tunic and a bearskin, and march up and down outside Buckingham Palace.

'Oh well' said the sergeant, 'as long as you know what you are letting yourself in for, sign here.' I told him I'd have to give my notice in at Sainsbury's which would be two weeks, and he instructed me to return at the end of that time when he would give me a railway warrant for the Guards Depot at Caterham. I left the recruiting office with my head held high and marched back to Bernard Jay Wallis.

The course was irrevocably decided. I had signed up for 4 years with the Colours and 8 on the Reserve. If the sergeant had suggested to me that as you're keen you ought to join up for the full 21 years, I'd have done so. Come to think of it had I done so I'd have only been 37 on leaving the army, and may have probably finished up as R.S.M.—though I somewhat doubt it with my brains—and at that age would have had a good pension and young enough to begin another career. They say that you have only one opportunity in a life time, but the number of favourable junctures I've had in mine is nobody's business.

Needless to say it was necessary to wait until Friday morning before I could speak to B.J.W. as he 'had gone to see a man about a dog' it being our half day off. Come the following morning and I sheepishly approached the great man to tell him what I had done.

'You've what?' he enquired.

I repeated what I had said. 'I'm going to be a guardsman so that I can wear a red tunic and a bearskin and march up and down outside Buckingham Palace to guard H.M. the King.'

'You silly bugger,' he said, 'you're not old enough. They'll put you in goal when they find out that you've lied to the Government. Never mind, I'll come and visit you.' This suggestion had me worrying for some considerable time, as being quite naive I felt there must be some truth in what he had said.

'Anyway,' I said, 'I've done it now, haven't I, and signed up.'

'Yes' he said 'you've cooked your goose and are in a lot of trouble, don't ask me to bail you out because I shall most likely have to go and see a man about a dog!'

'Trouble or not' I replied, 'I've got to give you two week's notice as I have to report back to Sergeant Richards in two weeks time, or a week on Monday.'

'Right,' said B.J.W., 'make sure you spend the rest of your time here on your hands and knees cleaning this place up; it's filthy. I don't know what you've been doing since you've been here.'

'Yes Sir,' I replied, feeling confused and not quite sure what I'd got myself in for.

The next two weeks seemed to drag on for ever, during which time I was employed for the greater part in my usual chores of cleaning the cold store and boning briskets, but to ease the pain, in the back of my mind I was on sentry duty doing 20 paces to the right and 20 to the left with my opposite number outside Buckingham Palace.

I made a couple more visits to the area during my days off, but this time discovered another route to avoid Piccadilly, arriving by tube at Marble Arch and walking down through Hyde Park to Hyde Park Corner and then on along Constitution Hill. On a Sunday morning I arrived in time to watch the changing of the guard witnessed also by a multitude of tourists, which convinced me, whether I was going to jail for misleading the Recruiting Sergeant or not, that I had made the right decision.

Once again, it did not occur to me that I should visit my father and mother for the weekend prior to my joining the Grenadier Guards. I could have quite easily arranged to spend a couple of days with my Mother and Father, but could not have told them what I had done. Even so, no sooner had I set foot inside Caterham Barracks in Surrey than my dear Mother shopped me. She had, by the way, lost a brother, Uncle Charley, shot off a horse in the Boer War. She wrote to the Prime Minister, Mr Stanley Baldwin, saying that I was only 16 and that he was to send me home to 'mummy and daddy' because I had been a naughty boy and told a lie about my age.

4
To be a Grenadier Guard: 1936 - 1946

Having spent barely three months as a trainee butcher, I took leave of Bernard Wallis, requesting that he should convey my sincere thanks to Mr Sainsbury and apologies for having to leave his employ so soon, but that I preferred the possibility of wearing a red tunic and a black bearskin instead of a white cap and apron which was not quite so glamourous. B.J.W. wished me well and said 'the only way you'll be able to change your mind during the next four years is to work your ticket.'

At the time I hadn't the faintest idea what he meant, until I saw someone standing in the middle of the parade ground taking the magazine out of his rifle, putting it on the ground, and marching round it. When the Regimental Sergeant Major asked him what he was doing he replied that he was 'on Magazine Guard, Sir.' The recruit was unsuccessful in his bid to leave the army and was instead escorted, at the double, to the Guardroom, one would assume for his own safety, and put under close arrest. The following day he was marched before the Commanding Officer and given 14 days jankers—confined to barracks with extra drills, at the double, three times a day. He never did a 'Magazine Guard' again. He had obviously been ill-advised by someone.

The Recruiting Sergeant presented me with the King's Shilling on April 10, 1936, together with my railway warrant for Caterham and wished me good luck in my future career. I arrived at the gates of the barracks some time before lunch, having taken rather a long time to pluck up sufficient courage to approach them. The Sergeant on guard beckoned me to follow him into the Guardroom where I presented him with the envelope containing my enlistment papers.

'Right, Jay' said the Sergeant, in a not too endearing tone of voice, 'stand there while I get the inlying piquet to take you down to the reception room.' In a short while the piquet arrived, having been on another errand, and the Sergeant ordered him to 'take this young man, Jay [you are always addressed or referred to by your family name unless you are an N.C.O., Non Commissioned Officer] in quick time down to the reception room.' The piquet took off at something like 130 paces to the minute and left me standing at least 50 yards behind, which resulted in the piquet having to mark time until I caught up with him. He muttered something like 'get a bloody move on, otherwise I'll miss my dinner. Sensing that I might miss mine I did my best and we arrived with me still 20 paces behind. I joined several others who had also arrived at the depot that day—the Grenadier Guards must be a very popular regiment, thought I—and after reporting to the Sergeant on duty was informed that I was too late for dinner, but 'we'll try and dish you up with a good tea which will be at 5.30 p.m.' First lesson; never be late for anything in the army.

Because we had to wait until there were sufficient numbers to form a squad of 30 men, the half dozen of us were ordered to collect our bedding from the Quartermaster's Stores and to make our beds in a spare barrack room. We also had to collect our mess-tins, mugs, and cutlery. For the rest of that particular day we were shown round the premises by the Piquet Corporal and were allowed to spend half-an-hour in the N.A.A.F.I. canteen to partake, at our own expense, of a 'cha and wad'—army slang for tea and cakes acquired whilst on foreign service, probably in India or Egypt. We didn't get anything special for tea after all, just the enormous mug of golden, delicious tea which is something in which the army cook excels and bread and butter, cheese and jam. We were then allowed to return to our beds and relax for the rest of the day, and go to the N.A.A.F.I.

canteen later on where we could indulge ourselves in a game of table tennis, billiards or darts, none of which I had even seen let alone played. One of the recruits, when I told him I couldn't play, asked me if I had been brought up by the monks in a monastery! When I asked, 'What do they do then?' he lost patience and carried on playing billiards. I thought to myself I was out on a limb here, and went and had a meal of bangers, which was at least something with which I was familiar. I had to return to our barrack room and be in bed by 'lights out' at 10 p.m., and having had a busy day it wasn't long before I was fast asleep.

It seemed that no sooner had I fallen asleep than I was rudely awakened by the sound of a musical instrument, which I later discovered was called a bugle and which I learned to recognise by the words: 'get out of bed, get out of bed, you lazy bugger.' I soon realised that there was no turning over as the N.C.O. would burst into the room and whip the blankets off you. Reveille was at 6 a.m. and in the Grenadier Guards 6 a.m. is 6 a.m., not 6.05. Until we were formed into a squad, we were only required to wash and shave ourselves and be properly dressed in civilian clothes before going down to breakfast in the mess, after which we were to report to the Piquet Corporal who would detail us for the day's duties.

Our various fatigues included cleaning and scrubbing wherever it was required—I was back at Sainsbury's again—but this time we had someone breathing down our necks all day. One of our jobs was sweeping a parade ground as big as a five acre field! Another was lugging coal to the married quarters. As we were still waiting to form a squad, we were just the boys to do all the dirty chores and there was no way out of it. Little did I realise that I had many hours of square-bashing to do before I'd ever be allowed to set foot outside Buckingham Palace.

After two weeks of this we were able to form a squad and were forthwith issued with our uniforms plus everything down to our underwear and socks, all of which were thrown out of the Quartermaster's Stores in our direction. As we were all about the same height and weight there was apparently no need to be measured for anything, and it was just hard luck if something did not quite fit. The only thing I was rather fussy about was my cap as I have a rather big head; it always has been the same size from as long as I can remember. At first they said that I would have to have a cap especially made, but by a stroke of good fortune they found me one at the back of the stores. Having been kitted out we were hauled off to our quarters for the next 16 weeks, and I was allotted the bed in the left-hand corner, on which there were already two biscuits—mattresses—and what seemed like straw pillows; maybe not straw but certainly not duck down.

First we were shown how to make up our beds into what appeared to look like armchairs with folded blankets and sheets. We then had to go into the armoury where we were issued with our rifle, a Lee Enfield .303, and bayonet, which we placed in its stand at the right of our beds. Our Squad Instructor was L/Sergeant Frank Dowling, and our Trained Soldier was T.S. Grogan, the latter of whom was an extremely kind and helpful person. To prepare for the following arduous day we were to make our beds down so that we could be initiated into the Shining Parade which consisted of sitting astride the bed and polishing our buttons and boots, the toes of which were polished to such a degree that it was possible to see your face in them. At the same time we had to begin learning regimental history and battle honours by heart. You were not allowed to do little rings on your toe caps with a blank mind, or to think how nice it would be to be with your favourite girl friends!

It was as I sat on my bed shining the toe caps of my boots for the first time, that Sergeant Dowling came up to me and said that my Mother had been in touch with the powers that be and told them that I was too young to join the army. 'You've got two choices, either to go home and face the wrath of your parents, or stay here and do extra fatigues. What do you want to do?'

Not knowing what 'extra fatigues' were at the time I replied 'I'll stay here Sergeant.' Extra fatigues mean doing odd jobs whilst your mates are scoffing—eating—bangers and mash in the N.A.A.F.I. canteen. I never did any, anyway. I didn't give it another thought until many years later, but I must have caused my parents a lot of anguish. They've gone, but one suffers for it for a long time.

When Reveille blew we had to scramble out of bed, pick our blankets up and run downstairs onto the barrack square to perform a parade called blanket shaking, not to remove the fleas, because there weren't any, but to freshen them up, and after shaking the blankets thoroughly for ten minutes we folded them up and ran back upstairs. We would then make our beds and proceed to the wash-house to wash and shave in cold water, then get properly dressed in our canvas clothing before attending Breakfast Parade. Here we would be inspected by the squad instructor to make sure we had washed and shaved properly—everybody had to shave even if your face was only covered in bum fluff! I'm sure our squad instructor hadn't been shaving for long, because he had a face as smooth as a baby's bottom. The parade was also to ascertain that our boots were highly polished. After the parade we were dismissed and allowed to go to the mess for breakfast, which was not to last for more than 20 minutes, after which we returned to our quarters and dressed for drill parade in our uniform with our equipment blancoed and polished thoroughly. We then went through intensive drill parades and at first had to be taught step by step what the motions were, because naturally we hadn't the vaguest idea what most of the commands meant, except for probably 'Attention.' But for commands such as 'Stand at ease', Right turn', and 'About turn' each step had to be demonstrated by the Squad Instructor. We were formed up in fours so that the command 'Dress to the right' was frequently necessary; as you can imagine the columns would some-times be inclined to form the shape of a boa constrictor. In retro-spect it must have been very trying for our instructor who must have had more than his share of patience. Once we had been drilled in the rudiments and basic moves our instructor began chasing us from one end of the parade ground to the other, until the sweat dropped off us. This was more from nerves, much the same as young horses being broken in, than exertion, because we were all fit men before we joined up, though not as fit as we were going to be. At any moment each of us expected our names to be called out for being inattentive or idle, and frequently the instructor would bellow, 'Webb, pick your feet up and swing your arms you are not on a Sunday afternoon's stroll', or 'Jay, you are not following the plough now, hold your head up and pull your shoulders back, and don't look at me otherwise I'll have you in double time into the Guardroom.' After an hour of this we'd be dismissed at the double, and told to return to the barrack room and change into gym kit— white vest and blue shorts with gym shoes—and go at the double to the gymnasium for physical exercises—we'd not had enough for the last hour. This included leaping over the wooden horse, though I never had the courage to jump being always afraid that I was going to fall and crush my crown jewels, and so only crawled over. It was quite simple really, all one had to do was place one's hands on top of the 'horse' and jump with legs astride and you'd normally land on the other side, but no matter what the P.T. Instructor threatened me with I never had the guts to try. The word was unheard of in those days, but I was, I suppose, a real wimp. After the P.T. exercises such as knees bend and press-ups, we were dismissed and returned to our quarters to prepare for another parade before dinner.

This may have been a musketry parade, so that we were required to change back into our uniform—we were quick change artists as well—and doubled out onto the parade ground to go through the motions of musketry drill with the Lee Enfield which, compared with the modern SA88, was a doddle. Unless I am mistaken the Lee Enfield comprised of three pieces, the main weapon plus the bolt and magazine. We were provided with a 'pull through' and a four by two with which to clean the barrel. If it was ever found to be dirty you were for the high jump.

On some days we were marched to the firing range and were allowed to practice with a .22. After we'd had some practice the instructor suggested that we have a competition and ordered us to put a penny into a kitty. The recruit with the highest score would be pronounced the winner, and be rewarded with the kitty. One of my mates once won the kitty, but by pure accident as the chap next to him must have been cross-eyed and scored a bull on my friend's target, giving him the highest score.

From musketry drill we returned again to our quarters where we'd leave our rifles, and proceed to dinner in the mess where the Trained Soldier would sit at the head of the table and dish out the grub to the 30 or so men in the squad, seated equally on each side of the trestle tables. We were only allowed one helping of dinner each, and one helping of duff—pudding—although after all the exercise we had done that morning we could have scoffed enough for a dozen men. We were always hungry as young men are, but we were more so because we did so much drill and physical exercise. After dinner we'd have to clear up the tables and sweep out the mess room. No food was ever dropped on the floor. Having performed this chore we again returned to the barrack room, and if we had time had a breather for five minutes before resuming our training programme.

At 1.30 p.m. we might have a Swimming Parade where we would learn to swim in the pool, and thank the Lord we did, because it stood us in good stead at Dunkirk a few years later when we had to swim for it. I only every learned to do the breast stroke, and sometimes to try and show off I'd swim on my side and shoot out my right arm to give the impression that I was doing the crawl. Actually I don't think I fooled anyone. After the Swimming Parade we might have Religious Instruction with the Padre or Chaplain depending on your denomination, or we might have School Parade. Oh yes, we had to go to school unless we had a School Certificate, and very few of us did. At the depot we had to go to school every other day, but when we arrived at the battalion we went to school every day.

Time for tea, and at 5.30 or 6 p.m. Shining Parade astride our beds again and learn our battle honours. If we'd got any money left we could then go to the N.A.A.F.I. for a tea and wad.

One of the tasks we completed was to mark all our possessions with our number. Every single thing had to be stamped, including your knife, fork and spoon, and on a Kit Inspection Parade all of it had to be laid out on your bed. One obvious reason was that if anything was lost it could easily be recovered should anyone have it by mistake!

As well as Kit Inspections we had a Body Inspection, having to stand on our beds in bare feet, naturally, and the Squad Instructor would have to inspect our hands and feet at least once a month after Shining Parade and after we'd been in the bathhouse. One of the first things to be performed, of course, would be to get a decent hair cut. You wouldn't be considered a clean and healthy looking specimen if you had long hair, though to most of us it wasn't a problem, as we had always had regular hair cuts.

Our wages were 2/6. a week at the depot, which might sound ridiculous at 12.5p a week, but you'd be surprised how far it went, especially if you didn't smoke or drink. You'd probably get more enjoyment, in the long run, out of taking a girl to the pictures or a dance, which would cost you a tanner (2.5p). I don't think I drank anything except tea at the time, but if we had a drink of beer, a pint would cost you 4d. Woodbine cigarettes cost 2d for five, there were five in a packet, and ten players cost 6d, so it was much more enjoyable to keep your money in your pocket, not smoke or drink, and take your girl friend to the pictures or a dance. If you were lucky you might score. One of our boys, Tommy Taylor, used to go out with his dance pumps on and go over the wall, it is alleged, because he couldn't go out through the gate with them on, though why he couldn't have carried them under his arm I don't know. We were first allowed out of the depot when we had done three months training, and were allowed out from 6 p.m. until 10 p.m. We had one weekend off in three months, but I can't remember if I went home. I most likely did, because it would have cost me more to go elsewhere, despite the train fare.

During one particular Shining Parade, which lasted from two to sometimes three hours, I must have been insubordinate to our Squad Instructor, because he sent me into the wash house where I remained for an hour thinking he was coming to beat me up at any moment, but T.S. Grogan came to tell me that I was to return to my bed. It never happened again, probably because when the opportunity arose I entered a boxing competition for novices and never having had the gloves on in my life before, hadn't the faintest idea of the finer points of the art. Being about 12 stones, or 168 pounds, I was entered as a light heavyweight and with my arms going in all directions, and whirling like a windmill, I caught my unfortunate opponent in the larynx and he fell to the canvas, trembling in every limb as though suffering from a fit. The M.O. was called and the orderlies removed the poor chap on a stretcher to the nearest hospital, where he remained for the next fortnight. I was so upset by what had happened and was afraid he was going to snuff it, so I visited him every other day, with special permission from the Commanding Officer. Fortunately, after a week he began to pull round and was able to eat a light meal of fish and mashed potatoes, and the Sister on the ward gave him permission to get out of bed for a couple of hours. He swore he'd never enter the ring again, but neither did my Squad Instructor send me into the wash house again!

Soon after I joined the battalion at Chelsea the squad were shocked to see their old Squad Instructor marching across the parade ground without his stripes. It transpired that he had been busted for striking a recruit. Being a good soldier though, and probably having learned his lesson, he was soon promoted and finished up as an R.S.M.

As soon as we formed a squad our sporting talents were noted so as to engage the recruit in his particular sport on the field. Because of my attempt to become a long distance runner I duly put my name down for that sport, together with boxing. They became my main interests during my service in the Guards. For some unknown reason I did not develop cauliflower ears or a flat nose as a result of my involvement in boxing, but I still have a memento four inches long on my right thigh as a consequence of becoming entangled in a barbed wire fence during a three mile run across country. It was perfectly ordinary barbed wire, not the razor sharp barbed wire of today, but nevertheless, probably due to my carelessness, left me with quite a gash resulting in a considerable loss of blood by the time

I completed the course, coming in third in a battalion of a thousand men. My right leg was covered in blood which prompted one of the officers to enquire as to whether I had hurt myself. 'Just a slight scratch, Sir.' I replied, but he thought it would be advisable that I report to the Medical Officer who arranged for me to have a blood test and transfusion, whereupon I was topped up with three points of blood. But they didn't award any medals!

Apart from our training programme we were frequently required to carry out a number of fatigues, or soldier's non-combatant duties, as the Ministry of Defence was loath to employ outside help to perform such chores as peeling potatoes when there were hundreds of able-bodied men to do it for nothing. So spud bashing was sometimes one of the details, with a number of men being ordered to report to the cook house and the squad instructor selecting some of his favourites. I was always chosen because I was the youngest in the squad and considered to be the most insubordinate—you'd only got to glance with your eyes without turning your head to be insubordinate—but never mind, we always got a lovely mug of golden tea at the end of the 'bashing'.

The piquet and defaulters (soldiers guilty of military offences) would parade in front of York block each time the drummer sounded for them.

Part of our training consisted of bayonet practice in which we were to charge at a bag of straw tied between two posts, scream at the top of our voices like a lot of savages, and thrust our 18" bayonets into the middle of the bag and out again quickly before moving on to the next victim, being careful you didn't stab your next door neighbour in the process by mistake. This is what you'd be doing whilst in battle with the French Imperial Guard on the battlefields at Waterloo during your sleep if you were the impressionable type such as myself.

Having been passed with flying colours by the Commandant at the depot, we were transported from Caterham to Chelsea Barracks together with all our kit, less our bedding (we didn't have to take our beds either) and taken to our barrack room on the second floor of a block, in which there were fifteen beds up each side of the room. I was detailed to occupy the sixth bed on the right-hand side. The sergeant did not say 'would you kindly take over this bed' he said 'you will sleep there.' We were then told to report to the Quartermaster's Stores and collect our bedding and returned to make our beds down for the night. We had missed our tea having been delayed by an over-turned vegetable lorry on its way to Covent Garden, so did the only sensible thing and spent our last few coppers on bangers and mash and a huge mug of tea in the N.A.A.F.I.—thank the Lord for it. It proved to be a life saver in more ways than one.

We were rudely wakened the following morning by the bugler playing the familiar tune on his bugle 'get out of bed, get out of bed, you lazy bugger' and the platoon sergeant bursting through the barrack room door at that very moment, screaming 'take your hands off it then, you're not at the depot now, you've grown up.' The routine was more or less the same, except that we were required to take part in ceremonial duties and as such were put through intensive foot drills on that enormous square, which did not deter either the Drill Sergeant or the R.S.M. whose voices carried from one side of the square to the other, especially R.S.M. Freddy Turner's, the smartest soldier in the British Army.

The first guard I ever did was on Buckingham Palace and there are not many who can say that they did sentry duty outside Buckingham Palace at the age of 16 during the reign of Edward VIII. Actually the King did not spend much time at Buckingham Palace, he more or less lived at Fort Belvedere, in Sunningdale near Ascot, and was seldom seen at the Palace unless he came to visit his mother, Queen Mary, whose main residence it was. Nevertheless, I had the honour of presenting arms to Edward VIII on the occasion I was selected for the guard, so not only did I achieve my ambition of strutting up and down the pavement outside Buckingham Palace, but I also had the honour of saluting the King. He was being chauffeured in his Rolls Royce and was alone. I don't think Mrs Simpson ever accompanied the King to the Palace, but she did stay at The Fort.

Our guard was of a 24 hour duration where, apart from being fed with food fit for a King, we were served with innumerable mugs of lovely, steaming hot, golden tea. You would 'do' two hours on guard and four off, so that every time you came off you would be handed a lovely mug of tea. Imagine what that meant at 2 in the morning. We had our photographs taken a number of times by the tourists and were dated frequently by lusciously developed young ladies from foreign countries, but as we were forbidden to even blink an eye, let alone utter 'yea or nay' many opportunities were, sadly, lost and we never learned whether it was because of the bearskin and the red tunic, or the magnificent specimen of manhood inside them!

We marched from Chelsea Barracks to the Palace, timed so that the Changing of the Guard took place at 11 a.m. on the Sunday, when the tourists would be congregating outside the railings to observe the great spectacle. We were accompanied by the Regimental Band and were dressed in our red tunics and bearskins—with its white plume on the left—folded greatcoats and rolled capes. On completion we were marched back to Chelsea Barracks and had the rest of the day off to do whatever we wished, which meant you tried to get as far away from the barracks as possible in case you were nabbed for something 'in which to fill your time.'

After you'd been at the battalion for three months you'd be issued with a Permanent Pass, in my case from the 3rd Battalion Grenadier Guards, which stated that 'this Pass is valid for a "certain period" until the expiration of your Colour Service', with your rank and number, and that you had permission to be absent until 1 a.m. the following day, and that you also had permission to wear plain clothes when walking out of barracks and permission to wear shoes when walking out in uniform, sometimes in red tunic, but without the bearskin. We wore a peaked cap. The civvies that we were allowed to wear had to be dark, whatever colour, and we were obliged to wear a trilby. In retrospect it's not difficult to believe that around midnight when returning to the barracks we must have

46

looked a menacing bunch of gangsters to anyone not familiar to such a sight, especially in the days of Edward G Robinson, Paul Muni and George Raft. I preferred to wear uniform when walking out of barracks as it was easier to pick up a 'bit of stuff', usually when walking along West Carriage Drive through Hyde Park on a Saturday or Sunday afternoon. At least they knew who you were and where they could find you if you slipped up, which was most likely the reason why the girls preferred us to some non-descript. We invariably ended up by having a roll in the grass, euphemistically speaking. Although our pay had increased to 7/6d a week, plus additional tanners—6d—for promotion or educational certificates, it did not enable us to dine at the Savoy or dance at the Dorchester, but we could go to the Hammersmith Palais or the Lyceum in the Strand where we picked up some beauties. One girl, a Jewess, took me home for the evening, but every time I tried to get near her she screamed her head off. She said she'd been married to a boxer— he'd obviously been doing something else besides boxing, but I never found out what it was.

But, there were more serious things to do besides dallying with de goils. The R.S.M. had other plans as we had to rehearse for Trooping of the Colour which involved much 'square bashing' foot drill. We had been drilled in fours, but because of the increase in traffic on the roads it was decided to march in threes, so as not to take up so much space and this necessitated new movements and formations. Trooping the Colour is a magnificent spectacle, but for the chaps who take part it's a long day, sometimes without food and drink for hours on end. It is not surprising that one might collapse from an empty stomach, or the stress or strain of standing about for hours on end doing nothing. Fortunately I didn't. If you did faint, you stayed there until the medics arrived, no one was permitted to give you a leg up.

Whilst I was stationed at Chelsea Barracks we had the good fortune to do a Guard on the Bank of England, which entailed marching to Sloane Square tube station, and travelling to the Bank Underground Station on the Tube and then undertaking a twelve hour Guard, or Nocturnal Guard, which involved two on and four off, marching up and down the corridors. We had the usual Guardroom where we slept, on and off—more off than on with heavy army boots on tiled floors clattering about the place—ate our meals and were served with the usual lovely mug of golden delicious tea, as only Grenadiers can make. For this we received a new shilling and I regret tremendously that I spent it almost immediately. What a lovely souvenir it would have been, but a shilling was a shilling and a lot of money which you couldn't afford to have making a hole in your pocket. A shilling was the entrance fee to the Astoria Ballroom in Charing Cross Road where you could dance to the likes of Jay Wilbur and Harry Roy, two of the best bands in the land.

From Chelsea Barracks we were moved to Victoria Barracks at Windsor to take over ceremonial duties on the Castle. By this time we had a new King and Queen who sometimes spent their weekends there, and on one occasion had the good fortune to be doing a Guard whilst they were in residence. We were also used to escorting tourists round the Castle, to make sure they did not stray into the forbidden territory; didn't wander into the dining room whilst the Royal Family were having their lunch!

It was during our stay at Windsor that I pursued my favourite sport, boxing, influenced by some of our great boxers, some of whom trained at the Star and Garter in Windsor, such as Len Harvey, Eric Boon, Dave Crowley, Freddie Mills and the German, Walter Neusel, who had been the scourge of British Heavyweights until Tommy Farr knocked him out in the second round. Len Harvey was one of the most scientific fighters and it was a pleasure to watch him training in the gym. He was World Light-Heavyweight Champion from 1939 - 1942, British Middle, Light-Heavy and Heavyweight Champion between 1929 and 1942, when he was knocked out in two rounds by Freddie Mills. He was a master of the art of self-defence, but slipped up in his last fight!

We were busily engaged in our training programme at this time for the Battalion Boxing Championships, so it was always an inspiration to see professionals training at the Star and Garter and we had the privilege of being able to use the Windsor Great Park for road work, being careful not to run down the Royal Family on the way round. We were quite a large group altogether. This had to be done in our own time as we were not the Battalion Boxing Team training for a match with another regiment. I was still a light-heavy, just, about 12 stones, and reached the finals. L/Cpl Ship, I'm afraid I've forgotten his Christian name, was by far the superior boxer. He, in fact, was a superb boxer with many years experience and at least 10 years older than I was, who at 17 was bursting with uncontrolled energy, not knowing where my fists were going to land. But by sheer brute force and aggression I won the day on points, avoiding as much as possible his larynx, though that was pure good fortune. Ship must have been a very disappointed man as he was so very good, but unless you can catch a novice on the chin as long as he has the stamina to keep going with his arms and fists, and persists in boxing forward he will win on aggression and points.

Our idol at this time was Tommy Farr, the great Welsh British and Commonwealth Heavyweight Champion, who on August 30, 1937, was to fight the 'Brown Bomber' at Madison Square Garden. Tommy Farr came from Tonypandy in Wales and he began boxing at 13 years of age, when he fought in travelling boxing booths on a Saturday night. He became Welsh Light-heavyweight Champion four months after his 19th birthday. The following year he moved into the heavyweight class and won his second Welsh title by knocking out Jim Wilde in seven rounds. Six months later Farr became Champion of Britain by out-pointing Ben Foord. After out-pointing the former World Heavyweight Champion Max Baer, and knocking out Walter Neusel, he got his big chance. Joe Louis had just become World Champion and Farr was appointed his first challenger. No Briton had fought for the world heavyweight crown for nearly 30 years and boxing fans throughout the United Kingdom got up in the early morning at 4 a.m. to listen to the radio. We couldn't have the lights on in the barrack room, but crouched round the solitary radio to listen to the fight. Farr fought like a tiger and forced the pace making the formidable 'Brown Bomber' back off.

But Louis fought back and won on points, though only just. We were sadly disappointed because Farr had done so well, and going the full distance which is more than could be said for 22 of the 'Brown Bomber's' opponents who were knocked out.

Back to reality and foot drill, weapon training and physical training. Once we marched from Windsor to Pirbright, roughly 20 miles, a mere stroll, at 2.5 miles an hour. We arrived at Pirbright Camp at 3 a.m. in time to have a couple of hours sleep before breakfast, before spending a day on the firing range. My hands were so unsteady that each time I fired the shot hit the outside ring, and once hit the target next door. We really should have had the day off after the forced march, but schedule is schedule in the army. However, we were allowed to rest before the return march the next night, but our platoon officer, Lt. Clive, got lost in Windsor Great Park about 1 a.m. and it was difficult to find our way out with the multitude of pathways. After much probing this way and that, we eventually arrived at Victoria Barracks at 2.30 a.m. but the cooks didn't get up to make us a cup of tea! Most, if not all, of us were so dead tired that we were asleep before hitting the sack. Our Commanding Officer very kindly took pity on us and gave us the following day off. An old friend of mine, by the name of Snell, and I went off to Slough for the afternoon and picked up a 'couple of dames' with whom we spent an agreeable afternoon on the banks of the River Thames, picnicking on some brown ale and fruit pies. Snell's girl-friend's photo appeared on the front page of the *Daily Mail* the next day, and we read that she had eloped with a South American polo player who'd been playing in the park the previous day. He was very cut up about it and wouldn't go out for a month, and my girl said she didn't want to go out by herself. I told her she wouldn't be by herself, that she'd be with me, but she said she didn't trust me on my own. The truth of the matter was that she wanted to elope with a polo player!

5
To be A.W.O.L.

In 1938 we moved to Barrosa Barracks at Aldershot where we spent much of our time in field training and what we squaddies referred to as playing silly buggers; war games out in the country, crawling about on our stomachs pretending to capture one another. This was something I did not relish, I'm ashamed to admit, so just before we were due to do another three or four days of camping under the moon and stars, I went A.W.O.L. and took off again for 'the big smoke.'

After taking the train from Aldershot to Waterloo I found myself in the centre of Soho in the West End of London and, planning on a long stay, I rented a flat just off Leicester Square. I found myself a job in the centre of Soho as a doorman/bouncer in a discreet strip-joint, where the pay was 30/- (£1.50) a week. My job consisted of showing the door to any unruly customer and barring any rowdies from entering, as it was a very intimate, well run establishment.

All went well until one afternoon when I was walking along Frith Street I passed a couple in a doorway who were having a heated discussion. The man was striking the young lady about the face, something I had never seen in my life before and which quite annoyed me to say the least. Feeling that I should come to the young lady's defence I turned round and walloped the man, felling him to the pavement where he remained, which was a silly thing to do in a place such as Soho where I was a comparative stranger, but being a naive idiot and not as street-wise as my fellow citizens, I did the only thing that any gentleman would have done. The lady who, 30 years later I decided must have been on the game, immediately linked arms with me and we marched up the street leaving the bully spread-eagled on the ground. I had to leave the young lady to her own devices as I was on my way to work, but by a strange coincidence we met up the following day and were having a cup of coffee in a cafe in the same area, when suddenly Anne cried out saying 'run for it, they're coming after you.'

I looked out through the open door and sure enough there were about half-a-dozen of them, including Anne's pimp, heading for the cafe. With a 20 yards start I ran towards Soho Square as fast as my legs could carry me, but not fast enough; by the time I got to the south-east corner of the square they were on top of me and I woke up with a badly bruised and swollen right eye and Anne standing over me. Apparently, I'd put up quite a fight, which was a natural reaction for a boxer I suppose, but not having much chance against such enormous odds. Anne told me later that I was lucky to get away with a black eye as the leader of the gang had done time for manslaughter and was a well known criminal. Anne kindly made arrangements with the proprietor of a nearby restaurant for me to have a wash and brush up, and slapped a piece of steak from the fridge onto my eye. By this time the police had arrived and miraculously had already arrested my attacker, and we were both carted off to Bow Street Police Station, charged with being drunk and disorderly, and locked up in separate cells for the weekend. Anne came to visit and said she was going to get Johnny, a Chinaman, to get me out, but he never showed up. My adversary had meanwhile suggested that he would pay the fines for both of us, which was jolly generous of him, wasn't it?

Whilst I was waiting to see the beak on Monday morning, an Irishman gave me the key to his flat in Maida Vale and told me that I'd find a bag of counterfeit coins—half-crowns and two shilling pieces—and like a silly nincompoop I fell for it.

TO BE A.W.O.L.

During this time I hadn't been in touch with my parents, because that would have been the first place the Military Police would have looked for me or asked questions. Years later, when it came out that I had been absent from the regiment Mother remarked that she thought I had been, and laughed. I think she was rather pleased as she had not wanted me to join up in the first place. At the time I am sure she must have been worried not to have received a letter from me. It's a long time, but I still have a guilty feeling inside me, even though Mother has been dead and gone for 25 years. I wish some of the young people of today would realise the heartache they cause their parents.

There was no need for me to take up the offer of the Irishman, who had been on the whisky the night before and must have been suffering from alcoholic poisoning as his lips were swollen, his eyes bloodshot and he couldn't keep his hands still, but I was intrigued and collected the imitation coins from his flat. He had suggested I should change them in the tube station machines at Tottenham Court Road, or any other for that matter. My friend Anne had mysteriously disappeared, some saying that she had gone home to her parents and others that she had emigrated to the States in fear of her life, but I had other friends besides, two of whom had run away from their home in the South-west. One was a lesbian, the daughter of a country parson, and the other was her girlfriend, and I invited them to join me in changing the counterfeit money. No sooner had we begun than several plain clothes policemen appeared; they had been propping up the pillars surrounding the change machines, waiting for us, probably as a result of the previous night's activities by the Irishman. He had shopped us indirectly and we were invited to accompany the policeman to Bow Street, where we were charged with using counterfeit coins. The following morning we were up before the magistrates. The two girls were given two years probation and sent home, and I was remanded in Brixton for a week because I had decided to report that I had gone A.W.O.L. The girls left without as much as a by your leave, regretting that they had ever set eyes on me, and I was taken to gaol where I remained under lock and key for a week, only being let out for an hour a day to exercise with the other prisoners in the exercise yard. The rest of my time I lay on my bunk awaiting the arrival of meals and lights out. I had nothing to read, not even the Bible.

A week later I was returned to Bow Street Magistrates Court where I was handed over into the safe keeping of an officer and a two man escort, with great relief as you can imagine. Thank God for the Army. You might want to get away from it for a time, but it was lovely to be back under its protection. The officer was asked if the Grenadier Guards were prepared to 'take this horrible man back into the regiment' and as soon as he had replied in the affirmative we were marched out into a taxi and transported to Waterloo Station. Back at Barrosa Barracks I was put under close arrest; but was given a lovely mug of hot, sweet, golden tea.

The following day I was marched before the Commanding Officer and given 28 days in the 'glasshouse'; the army prison in Aldershot. (It has since been demolished as being beyond modernisation). When I was marched out of the C.O.'s office and standing between my escort awaiting transport, an officer came up to me floating on a cloud of perfume and said 'It was a girl, wasn't it Jay', to which I replied 'Well it wasn't a boy, Sir.' His response was to scream at the top of his voice, 'Put him in the book, Sergeant, for insubordination. We'll attend to him when he's done his 28 days.' The prison's regime was much the same as any other, except that we did drill at the double several times a day with full pack. When I entered the jail I weighed 12 stones, and when I was discharged I was 1 stone lighter, not because of a reduction in our diet, but because of the enforced drill. Perhaps it was good boxing training and one way to lose weight, something I had not been able to do before when I wanted to get down to middleweight.

Every morning after breakfast, which was brought round to each cell and put through the observation window in the door, the

Sergeant in charge of our section, about ten men, took us to the prison toilet and we would have to take turns to use it as there were only six toilets available. After about three minutes the Sergeant would shout 'Come on you blokes, nip it off, you're not supposed to sit there all day.' Once when we were marching back to the cells the Sergeant reproached me for being too long. I tried to explain that I had a slight problem to which he replied that I'd have to do extra drill at the double.

However, we survived and with a few days' remission for good behaviour, I was back with the battalion in Barrosa Barracks in no time and was ordered to fall in with the battalion boxing team and do some road work; this was no problem for me as I'd been doing plenty of it for the last three weeks or so. After a while the Sports and Entertainments Officer came to see me and informed me that I would be fighting the European Police Middleweight Boxing Champion at New Scotland Yard. As I had put on a bit of weight again, it was arranged that we go to the Russell Square Turkish Baths to remove the excess flab. This was hardly necessary as I could have got it off by doing some heavy road work with full kit, but in the army, at least under the rank of L/Cpl, you are not allowed to think, you are told what to do; your opinion is not required. Anyway, the officer and myself went to the baths which was another experience for me and I spent an hour, without the officer, in the steaming hot bath where I lost the few pounds required and came out feeling as though I'd been locked up with two nymphomaniacs for a week. I was in no state to go three rounds with the European Police Champion. Fortunately, there was a gap of a week which gave me a little time to recover. For some reason or other it was supposed to be the main contest of the evening, so we had a long wait before we were due to enter the ring. The policeman, after we had been introduced, bounced out of his corner and I stopped him with a straight left and a right cross to the chin, whereupon he sank to the canvas on one knee. At the count of six he got up and circled the ring, shooting out his left to keep me at a distance and produced a hay making right to put me on my back, at which I was saved by the bell. The second round was spent sparring and wrestling with one another, each being afraid of being hit having both been put on the canvas. In the third round my opponent put me down twice and after struggling to my feet I lost on points, needless to say. I've always put this down to the Turkish Bath; it really does sap your strength though I realise we can't win them all.

As a reward for providing the entertainment I was given a long weekend pass, so stayed in 'the smoke' and visited my old stamping ground (I shall always love Soho) in anticipation of seeing another girlfriend, from British Guyana. On the Sunday morning, and before contacting Maria, because she'd had a late night and early morning at the strip joint, I called into the 'Black Duck' for a pick-me-up. Whilst I was standing in the far corner a George Raft type of character, wearing a trilby and with a cigar between his teeth came sauntering over to me and said 'If you don't stop dallying with my woman, Maria, I'll blow your effing brains out, you bastard.' I replied that I was sorry, but I didn't know she was his girl friend and that as far as I was concerned I had no intention of ever seeing her again. He said that somebody had told him whilst he was in the nick that I was 'knocking off his woman.' It was a long time before I ever returned to Soho! It's very sociable!

During our stay at Barrosa Barracks I was sent on a driving course and ended up driving a 15 cwt Bedford truck. But that is all I could ever do as I was hopeless when it came to anything mechanical, except changing the plugs—as long as I changed one at a time and didn't remove the other leads. I was not mechanically minded in the least and it proved my downfall some time later. However, according to a Company Pay Sergeant I met in later years I wasn't a bad driving instructor and he succeeded in passing his driving test. So apart from eventually instilling some discipline into me the army also taught me to drive.

Throughout the summer of 1939 the clouds of war were looming overhead and the crunch came on Sunday, 3 September, at

11.15 a.m. I was sitting in the N.A.A.F.I. canteen having a tea and wad, having just done a two hours on and four off on the Barracks Guardroom, and so was excused Church Parade, when the Prime Minister, our dearly beloved Neville Chamberlain, made his dramatic announcement:-

I am speaking to you in the Cabinet Room from 10 Downing Street. This morning the British Ambassador in Berlin handed the German Government a final note stating that unless we heard from them by 11 o'clock that they were prepared to withdraw their troops from Poland, a state of war would exist between us. I have to tell you now that no such undertaking has been received and that consequently this country is at war with Germany.

I shall never forget that experience. The canteen was full of squaddies listening to the broadcast, but as far as I was concerned I was the only one there, transfixed, dumbstruck and glued to the chair. The very first thought that came into my head was that I was going to die; I was only 19 and I was very frightened. I was no hero and I didn't think like someone I heard say recently 'right let's get at 'em and get it over with.' That is a load of pure bravura. I don't know how long it was before I removed myself from the chair and the canteen, I suppose I was in a daze and in another world fighting Jerry already, but eventually I proceeded to the mess hall for dinner filled with doom, dread and despair, and thence to our barrack room and spent the rest of the afternoon in the trenches, lying on my bed. That night in my dreams I was up to my knees in mud on the Somme slaying Germans left, right and centre.

We mobilised immediately and prepared to embark for France, but before doing so we were given five days leave, part of which I spent at home and the rest with some friends in London. One of them suggested that I accompany him to meet his girl friend who would have a friend with her, a nurse from the same Middlesex hospital. We rented a flat for a couple of days in Edgeware Road, bought a few bottles of wine and some bread and cheese, and the rest is history.

6
We Embark for France: 20 September 1939

The following day we reported back to our Battalion, after promising to keep in touch with the girls, and by the next weekend we were on our way to Brest. From there we travelled for some three days in cattle trucks to La Posterie, 15 miles to the south-east of Lille on the Franco-Belgian border, where we were billeted in some cowsheds. The Company Headquarters was billeted in Chateau du Fe about a kilometre up the road. We were there for seven months digging 6 ft trenches during a very cold, snowy winter that were never used, at least by us, and I doubt by anyone else. We didn't have time to stop in any trenches.

It was at La Posterie where my lack of mechanical knowledge dropped me in it. I was the Platoon Officer's driver of our 15 cwt Bedford, and he wanted me to take him to Company Headquarters. We had only gone a hundred yards when the engine stopped and I couldn't get it to go again. It transpired that the rotor arm was cracked, but I never dreamt of looking at the distributor head by removing the cap. Anyway, that was the end of my cushy driver's job for a while, though not long enough. It was back to the trenches digging with pick and shovel for the next couple of months. Periodically we had a kit inspection, just like old times and to keep us in practice, and to my horror someone had had the temerity to steal my emergency ration. It's impossible to lose a 2 lb tin of concentrated chocolate, but I was charged with losing it and was sentenced to ten days confined to billets which meant I could not go on one of our soirées to Lille to visit the girls at the social club!

We continued to dig and man part of the Gort Line during the winter of 1939/1940 but had some 'excitement' as some would call it in No Man's Land on the other side of the Maginot Line. It has always struck me as most peculiar that a patrol was formed mostly out of the battalion boxing team plus a few extras, as you needed more than boxing ability if you came up against a sub-machine gun. However, that was the case and we began doing training exercises for patrol in the territory beyond the Maginot Line.

A great degree of hospitality was pressed on us when we were stationed near Lille during our infrequent trips to the city and where we made straight for what we called the 'Social Club' in the centre of the town. My favourite was a girl from Martinique, then a French Colony, who was the colour of Café-au-lait with a strikingly beautiful body. There must have been a mutual attraction as it was very difficult to keep us apart!

Approaching Christmas 1939, the battalion decided to send out its talent scout, the Sports and Entertainments Officer, with a view to putting on a concert. Someone must have heard me warbling in the shower and had decided that I was good enough to take part, passing the information on to the afore mentioned officer, because the next thing I knew was that I received the following instructions:-'You are detailed to sing at the concert on the 31 December.' It being a Sunday and because I had been heard singing 'There's a gold mine in the sky far away' I was billed to sing Hillbilly songs. Not having a wide repertoire it was naturally included in my spot, together with 'Empty saddles in the old corral' and ' She'll be coming round the mountains when she comes'. I don't remember getting an encore! They more than likely shouted 'get him off'. It was the first time I had ever sung in public, never having been encouraged or made aware that I had the ability to sing. Usually someone recognises that a child, when young, has a voice and is invited to sing in a church choir. Unfortunately, there was no such choir in our church.

The New Year's Eve Concert was a huge success. One of the acts performed by Guardsman Wood was an impression of a woman having a bath and he was obliged to perform an encore (there were no ladies in the audience to embarrass). The rest of the 'artists' did exceedingly well considering they had little time for rehearsal. Guardsman Wright accompanied everybody on the piano and continued to do so whenever the opportunity arose throughout the war and afterwards, and I remember him accompanying me to sing for the nurses in the Cottage Hospital in Hawick, Scotland. He was a tremendously gifted pianist. There were rumours to the effect that an E.N.S.A. party was to provide some entertainment for us during this time, but they did not put in an appearance, neither then or at any other time throughout the war. We always provided our own amusements.

That winter was very severe and most of the time the ground was covered in snow. In February, after much field work, we were on our way to No Man's Land on the other side of the Maginot Line. We were billeted in a police barracks, the police having been evacuated, where we remained for three weeks. There were three patrols, one from each of the battalions in the Brigade, and we took it in turns, sometimes going out at night from 6 - 11 p.m. and other times from 1 - 6 a.m. Because of the snow we had to wrap our guns up in white cloth, making sure working parts were not impeded. Our tin helmets were covered in white cloth and we wore white wellington boots and covered our uniforms with white canvas jackets and trousers, over which we slung our white webbing with pouches filled with ammunition. Once we were within sight and sound of the Hun, we fell to the ground and crawled around very slowly on all fours, making as little noise as possible. We frequently heard the German scouts who'd been sent out in advance of their patrol making the sound of an owl, but so obviously artificial it must have been made with a whistle especially made for the purpose. Whenever this happened we would lie perfectly still until the danger had passed! We were not supposed to engage the Germans in combat at this juncture, but approach and try to learn the position and condition of our enemy. We were fortunate, despite what the heavy brass may say, that we did not come face to face with Jerry during one of their patrols, otherwise there would have been merry hell to play as we were armed to the teeth with tommy guns, rifles and bayonets, grenades and a bren-gun. Some of us had sheath knives for close quarter work.

One of the delights of being in this No Man's Land patrol was that we were provided with a ration of Barbados rum before we ventured forth into the night—because of the weather not for the Dutch courage—though there were times that we needed more than the tot of rum supplied before leaving the police barracks. During our off duty hours when we were not asleep, we spent a lot of time playing Pontoon, but not for money because we had none; there was nowhere to go and in any case they were saving it for us back at H.Q. so we could have a right rave up when we returned home to La Posterie, all 30/- of it!

On one occasion we had instructions to go out early one morning and occupy the abandoned village of Zuerange. Our brief was to remain in the village occupying the houses which had been left completely furnished—but they had forgotten to fill the kettle and there was no sign of the tea pot or the tea, and the beds were not made. We had to wait for the Germans to come down into the village to pick up a pig, which was their wont when they were short of meat, and capture them regardless of how many there were. We hoped they would not need more than just two or three men to catch a pig. Whilst we were waiting for these Germans, having posted a lookout discreetly, we had the task of searching the houses in the village, the object of the exercise being that we would enter through one door but never return through the same. Not forgetting that we were all dressed in white, like a lot of virgins, L/Cpl Harry Nicholls, a close friend of mine and the Imperial Services heavyweight boxing champion, being the independent spirit he was, wandered about all on his tod looking for the enemy. He suddenly appeared through a door coming from the opposite direction, and Sergeant Matty Hayes screamed ''Tis a German' to which Harry equally screamed back 'Don't shoot for Christ's sake, it's your old mate Harry Nicholls.' Harry lived to tell the tale and later win a V.C., but only just.

We waited all that day and half of the next night, but the Germans must have exhausted the porcine supply as they did not put in an appearance, much to our relief, though by this time we were famished and starving to death from the cold. We'd forgotten to bring our sandwiches and beer, and the inhabitants of the village hadn't left any provisions in their cupboards. As we were leaving the village on our way home, we rang the church bell to let the Germans know, and they replied by lobbing a few shells over our heads, but we reached our billets safely to enjoy our tot of rum and a hearty, well deserved, meal.

After three weeks of patrolling during which time we witnessed distant battles between other patrols, seeing the tracer bullets zooming through the air, we returned to our cowsheds in La Posterie. When we had had a good rest after our exhausting three weeks our most immediate plan, which we had been discussing incessantly during our periods of relaxation—your mind does not wander to the fairer sex when you have your eyes peeled looking for the enemy—was to make a foray, without delay, to the 'Social Club' in Lille where, as usual, we were showered with great hospitality and kindness! Ma cherie Marie always received me with open arms and abandoned anyone she happened to be entertaining at the time.

After our raid on the Social Club our next concern was to satisfy the inner man and we always placed the same order, because it was the only French we knew for ordering food and that was 'oeufs et pomme de terre frit, s'il vous plait, Mademoiselle.' The first French I learned was 'Voulez-vous promenade avec moi ce soir, Mademoiselle' and the next word was 'dormir' which incidentally is the same in Spanish and Portuguese so there's no problem! 'Vin du table' was ever present as anywhere else on the Continent; they drink wine like we drink tea.

Soon after our return from our tour I was transferred to the Brigade's anti-tank company as a driver for the platoon representing our battalion, of one of the 15 cwt Bedford trucks on which was towed a 25 millimetre brand new French gun manned by a Sergeant and four guardsmen. This was a bonus indeed; the Great Architect had his eye on me from the start.

So it was, that on May 10, 1940, when the Germans invaded Holland and Belgium, our battalion, together with the 1st Guards Brigade, a battalion of Coldstream Guards and a battalion of the Hampshire Regiment, with our Hotchkiss anti-tank guns now in tow, entered Belgium to meet the invading Germans. We drove through Brussels and onto the banks of the river Dyle where we remained until the Germans broke through at Sedan, whereupon we withdrew to avoid being cut off, on the night of 16 May, and moved every night for the next three nights until we reached the river Escaut where a tremendous battle ensued as I witnessed after crossing the bridge over the river, with tracer bullets being fired from both sides. That night six officers of the 3rd Battalion were killed, including the Duke of Northumberland, a lieutenant, together with over 80 other ranks.

Each night we moved about 20 miles, mostly driving without lights of any kind for fear of being bombed. The roads were choked with refugees with their belongings loaded onto carts, prams and every conceivable means of transport. There were dead animals lying on the sides of the roads which had been killed by strafing Stukas, the human beings having been removed by military ambulances. I could never understand why the Belgians or French left their homes in the first place. Where were they going, into the sea? They would all have to return to their homes in the end only to find that they had been looted, at the least. Once, when we were given a breathing space—how did that happen?—we stopped near some farm buildings where the cows were in the cowshed waiting to be milked, but the farmer and his family had flown; the poor cows were bursting to be milked, so I found a three legged stool and a milk pail and proceeded to relieve the poor old cows of some of their distress. In the midst of my milking, in walked Captain Richard Llewelyn of the Welsh Guards, author of *How Green is my Valley*, who was attached to our anti-tank company. When I explained that they would be getting a fever if they were not milked, he agreed that I was doing the right thing and said 'Well done boyo, you're doing a grand job.' I have often wondered what became of the cows and the family. The family hopefully survived and returned home, but I have my doubts about the cattle. They could very well have been slaughtered, shot on the spot to provide food for the German army.

We learned later of news of our colleague Harry Nicholls. *The London Gazette* dated 20 July 1940 read as follows:-

'On 21 May 1940, L/Cpl Harry Nicholls was commanding a section in the right forward platoon of his company when the company was ordered to counter-attack. At the very start of the advance he was wounded in the arm by shrapnel, but continued to lead his section forward; as the company came over a small ridge, the enemy opened heavy machine-gun fire at close range.

'Lance Corporal Nicholls realising the danger to the company, immediately seized a Bren gun and dashed forward towards the machine-gun firing from the hip. He succeeded in silencing first one machine-gun and then two other machine-guns, in spite of being severely wounded.

'Lance Corporal Nicholls then went on up to a higher piece of ground and engaged the German infantry massed behind him, causing many casualties and continuing to fire until he had no more ammunition left.

'He was wounded at least four times in all, but absolutely refused to give in. There is no doubt that his gallant action was instrumental in enabling his company to reach its objective and in causing the enemy to fall back across the River Scheldt. Lance Corporal Nicholls has since been reported to have been killed in action.'

It transpired, however, some months later that he was alive and had been taken prisoner. It was also rumoured that he had suffered 17 wounds. He was sent home on 9 May, 1945, to Nottingham and a hero's welcome. He had two brothers in the regiment, Joe played for Spurs and Bristol Rovers as goalkeeper and Jack was my second-in-command in the section in Tunisia. I once foolishly punched him on the nose because he brought my sister into the conversation, and have been sorry ever since for what I did and making a fool of myself. I once went to seek him out in Nottingham to apologise, but he had died. They are all dead now. Harry died aged 60 on September 11, 1975. Because it was thought that he had been killed his widow was presented with Harry's Victoria Cross by King George VI on 6 August 1940, but after his repatriation he himself was presented with it by His Majesty, the only time a Victoria Cross has been presented twice.

Harry was British Army Heavyweight Champion which he won at the Albert Hall, and Imperial Services Heavyweight Champion which he won at the Empress Hall, Earls Court, in 1938. If someone had put a bullet in the back of Hitler's head at an early stage in his career, Harry could possibly have been World Champion; he won all his fights on a knock-out with a hay maker that started from the canvas. Matty Hayes, who nearly put Harry's 'lights out', had an equally devastating left hook and could also have gone a long way, but he was afraid of getting his good looks knocked about! (As I've said we were all boxers except for a few professionals in the Special Patrol.)

A General, who shall remain nameless, wrote to me some time ago discussing an incident and suggested that after a period of 50 years our memories become nebulous. Maybe so for some people; I certainly couldn't remember anything from one minute to the next when I was at school, but there were incidents during the war that one is never likely to forget. Incidentally, Tom Flemming the B.B.C. narrator, recounted a story of the same General who reportedly asked a subordinate, 'Who was the stupid man who ordered the flags to be put up there?' referring to a slip road off the Mall in London. 'You sir,' came the reply. So much for clouded memories.

After our sojourn on the Belgian Farm, about May 22, we were ordered to withdraw and moved during the night. It was the start of the withdrawal to Dunkirk. We were put on half rations and for the last two days before reaching Dunkirk relied on our emergency rations.

I wrote the following letter in March 1990 to the *Daily Express*, part of which was published, in response to their request for reader's experiences at Dunkirk:

'During the drive in convoy to Dunkirk we were bombed by fifteen Junkers. They had been flying up and down the convoy several times and did not appear to have any markings on them; as they had been flying at about 500 feet and to the west of us by 100 yards without dropping any shit we, in the truck, the Sergeant and I, decided they were friendly flyers when on the last run they dropped their bombs in the fields; they obviously did not wish to destroy their means of communication by dropping the bombs directly on the road and us, but they still did a lot of damage. The Sergeant sitting in the passenger seat was severely wounded in the arm and getting out of the vehicle and walking round to the rear discovered that all four guardsmen had also been hit, one of them whose name I remember quite well, but for obvious reasons can't name, had a hole blown in his back the size of a football. This happened, by the way, on 24 May. Sergeant Petty had by this time arrived from a forward vehicle, he being the Platoon Sergeant, a Canadian by the way and a good heavyweight boxer. The badly wounded man whose eyes had been glazed at first sight was now unconscious and beyond remedy so that the first thing we did was to evacuate the wounded in an ambulance who, hopefully, were taken to a hospital ship. We then removed the by now dead man and placed him in a ditch and put a blanket over him. I hope someone found him and gave him a Christian burial. What I could never understand was why the convoy had not been stopped so that everybody could have got into the ditches. We were only travelling at a snail's pace in any case. Someone must have known that they were not Allied bombers. I don't think we had as many and the French machines were of varying degrees of obsolescence, and these planes were the first we had seen to date.

Thinking that my truck had been immobilised by the bombs and being in a state of shock myself, I jumped onto the back of the vehicle in front and proceeded to Dunkirk, or as we then thought to the coast - you never knew where you were going, you were just led by the nose, we certainly didn't know we were going to Dunkirk to be evacuated at that point - until we were ordered to abandon our trucks, first by taking the rotor arms out and destroying them, and to then make our own way to the port. Strangely enough I became separated from the main body of men which was just as well I later came to realise, and crossing a field all on my own, miraculously in the right direction as it turned out, I was brought face to face, though not literally, with a headless and limbless corpse. As it was some distance from the town, about 30 years later I decided that the victim must have been a fifth columnist or someone who had taken revenge at an opportune time as he, and it definitely was male, could not have been a crashed pilot being completely nude as well as being just a trunk without any identification.'

Since writing the above Max Vincent, the son of Frederick Vincent, rang me to say that he was the son of Frederick Vincent who was killed in my truck when on our way to Dunkirk, and that he was only 14 months old when his father died. By some miracle, which so far remains a secret, our friend ex-Sergeant George Webb who spent 30 years in the West Mercia Police, discovered that Frederick Vincent had a son and got in touch with him, suggesting that Max got in touch with me knowing that I had written a book and had mentioned the incident of the bombing in it.

I have always been concerned that Frederick Vincent had remained in the ditch where we had placed him, covering him with a blanket, but I am now relieved to know that through some phenomenon he was discovered, probably by the local inhabitants or even the Germans, and buried in the local cemetery. Later, according to Major J.P. Schellekens, Chairman of the Belgian Remembrance Fund, wrote Mrs W. Vincent a letter to say that her husband's remains had been moved to Adegem (near Brugge in Belgium) to the Canadian War Graves Cemetery on 12 January 1978. Major Schellekens also mentions that advice would be provided for travel and hotel reservation for Mrs Vincent and her son Max when they intended to travel to Adegem. He said they would also arrange for a religious service at the grave of Frederick Vincent, whose full name was Guardsman Frederick George Vincent, and his army number 2612591. He was killed according to the information on the gravestone on 18 May 1940. He was 28 years of age. Max, the son, has since returned to the cemetery and laid his mother's ashes to rest with her husband.

7
Dunkirk

Eventually I reached a beach completely deserted and certainly no part of the famous Dunkirk Mole, on the way sheltering under a railway goods carriage from the Stukas dive-bombing the beaches. Lo and behold, awaiting my arrival was the destroyer *Worcester*. This is what I say about the Great Architect—He was always there when I needed him and I'll guarantee that my dear Mother and Father were down on their knees praying for me at every opportunity. Another lost soul who had been guided in the right direction came sauntering along. Together we picked up a wounded man left on a stretcher by a wall and braved the Major standing at the top of the gang plank with a revolver in his hand who allowed us to pass with our wounded 'colleague'. In retrospect it is most peculiar that the *Worcester* was waiting on a deserted beach when from all accounts there were thousands of men queuing up on the Mole with no immediate hope of boarding a vessel of any kind.

We were indeed very fortunate in some respects, for we were dive-bombed and machine-gunned whilst we were waiting to weigh anchor. The *Worcester* was a sitting duck—actually it was a sitting destroyer and much bigger than a duck—but the Germans must have been on the binge the night before and couldn't see straight or hadn't had much practical experience, because the only direct hits were three bombs that hit the bow, but at such an angle that they just skimmed off into the sea and exploded at such a distance from the destroyer that they did no harm. However, one bomb did explode near the stern and a little chap who was sitting as near as possible to the edge of the deck got a piece of shrapnel that went right through his stomach and he died soon afterwards. I was standing behind a bofors gun, a light anti-aircraft gun, with a fellow grenadier when one of the screaming stukas came diving towards us with all guns firing and dropping his bombs. With the bofors firing at the same time as the Stuka, it was too much for our friend who put his arm round me and shouted above the din 'Jesus Christ Jay, save me.' What can you say in the circumstances? 'Don't worry old chap, I'll look after you?' All you can say is 'It's all right mate, they won't get us.'

At long last we pulled out and whilst the bombers chased us out a fair way, we only saw one solitary spitfire about half way between Dunkirk and Dover that provided us with an escort to the port. It was the only British plane I saw throughout the withdrawal and evacuation.

As we were arriving in the harbour of Dover the *Maid of Orleans*, belonging to the Southern Railway, crossed our bows and the *Worcester* crashed into its side. Four guardsmen, in full kit, went over the side. I didn't know any of them and don't know whether they were strong swimmers, but they would have to be being fully dressed and overladen with full packs. I do hope they made it and lived to tell the tale.

We finally disembarked and got a lovely mug of tea, with wad, from the W.R.V.S.—God bless them!

In my speech for my 70th birthday I said 'No one believes in war and if the pre-war parliamentary, political, parasitic pests had listened to Winston Churchill there wouldn't have been a war because Hitler's ambitions would have been nipped in the bud before he occupied the Rhine, but no one would listen to him not even some of his fellow Conservatives who heckled him across the benches in The House.' As a result of their dithering the British lost over 3,000 killed in three weeks prior to the evacuation, the French over 100,000 killed with 250,000 wounded, and 1,500,000 taken prisoner. If it had not been for Lord Gort, who won a V.C. in the

First World War commanding the 1st Battalion Grenadier Guards at the age of 32, who hastened the withdrawal and evacuation, some of us alive today would be six feet under in France or Belgium, and others would have been taken prisoner, This despite Churchill, our dear Prime Minister, sending a message to Lord Gort which said 'Of course, if one side fights and the other does not the war is apt to become somewhat unequal.' Churchill did not include this in his memoirs by the way. He must have known that the allied forces were 'up against it' with Hitler's Luftwaffe of 3,000 modern aircraft, ours of little over 250 and France's almost 1,000 antiquated machines.

The allied forces in contrast out-numbered the German tanks by 3,500 to 2,200, but instead of using them likes packs of pit bull terriers as the Germans used their Panzers, ours were dotted along the frontiers and scattered among the regiments. With our tanks in such numbers and used properly we could have been in Berlin for Christmas 1939, but we had no air power to back them up. The Germans had to stop their Panzer power about 20 miles from Dunkirk because they were too far ahead of the troops and fearful of being cut off, which gave us an opportunity to evacuate more troops, the final count being 330,000 including 120,000 French in the eight days between 28 May and 4 June. I, incidentally, left on 2 June thanks be to God!

We hadn't the faintest idea where we were going, as usual, when we arrived at Dover. But after the tea and wad, the first in two days—I'd die without a cup of tea every two hours today—we boarded a train which took us to Waterloo where we changed for Aldershot and a temporary encampment of bivouacs in a field, Laffan's Plain. From there we were sent on ten days leave and I arrived by train at Hereford railway station some time before 5 p.m. and was able to reach Mr Challoner's hardware shop just before he closed, in time to get a lift to Portway where he also ran a pub and where he invited me in for a drink, naturally enough. I must have been a queer customer, because at that age I was tongue-tied most of the time and with all I had been through during the last three or four weeks incapable of stringing two words together. I remember Mr Challoner, an old family friend, asked me if I'd just returned from Dunkirk and all I had said was 'Yes'. He might have asked me 'When?' and I would have replied 'Last Saturday.' 'Where did you disembark in England,' and I might have said, 'I am not sure, but I think it was somewhere in Kent, a place called Dover.' I was what you would call monosyllabic and as a person in a dream not quite knowing if we were living in a dream world.

After drinking a pint of beer and not forgetting that I had to go home to my parents who were strictly teetotal, I left the Challoner family, including their daughter Nora who was a fine pianist, and walked the mile or so to the cottage where Mother and Father lived with my brother Steve who was then about 16 years of age. As it was summer Mother was alone because Dad and Stephen were still out working on Uncle Bert's farm, Dad's brother's farm.

Dad had since lost his rented farm and Uncle Bert had kindly given him a job and a cottage in which to live, which I used to call the Corner House but I don't think it was its real name. I'm not quite sure why they lost their farm, but I think they ran into ever deeper financial difficulties.

I may have written to Mum and Dad to say that I would be coming on leave but quite likely had not, not knowing what the next move was going to be. They had no such thing as a telephone so I could not phone them, and being young and thoughtless, it never occurred to me to make inquiries and get the Challoners' telephone number so that I could have left a message to say that I had landed safely and would be seeing them some time in the near future. I had never used a telephone in my life and perhaps was not aware of their existence, so it may have come as a complete surprise to my Mother to find me on the doorstep. I don't suppose she threw her arms round my neck as neither of my parents were demonstrative in any way, except that my Mum turned the tap on quite often, which was something over which she had no control. But I don't think she did on that occasion; if she did, it was through the joy she felt at seeing me rather than of sadness—she wasn't likely to have said 'What the flippin' 'eck did you come home for?'

We were by now living on different planets so there wasn't much to talk about, not that we were ever very communicative. They never took a daily paper or had a wireless so they had no idea whatsoever what had been happening on the other side the water, and I was only capable of mumbling gibberish. They were just pleased to see me and thanked the Lord that I had survived whatever it was 'over there'. After a meal I walked back the half mile or so to the Portway where we had a sing-song with Nora on the piano, which is what I did practically every night, much to the dismay of my God fearing, teetotal parents, which is why I should call this book 'An Ungrateful Wretch'. Friends called for them in their cars to take them to their beloved church in Hay-on-Wye, but I never accompanied them once and no one had more motive than myself for getting down on my knees in church and thanking God for my deliverance. Of course I thanked God, but I did not demonstrate my love for Him as I should have done with my Mother and Father.

With Dad being a conscientious objector in the 1914-18 war he had no interest in what was happening, so that very little was said between us other than passing the time of day, and sometimes not even that. I suppose he thought that I had been frantically waving my rifle and bayonet about, shooting and stabbing people to death when in fact had he asked, I could have told him that I had not even seen a German apart from the ones leering at me out of their Stuka cockpits saying something like 'here's something for you my little friend.'

Being home on furlough and being able to potter about on my uncle's farm was a pleasant change from soldiering. It was where I would have been, no doubt, had I remained on my Uncle Leonard's farm at the Veldt House, if he had applied for me to be exempt from military service as he may have been short of staff on his dairy farm. On the other hand I have no regrets whatsoever for the decision I made. Very few people have led a more interesting life than myself, or seen so much of the world.

During the war everybody mucked in on the farm just for the pleasure of it. Cycling clubs biked for miles just to spend the weekends helping out on the farm, but the Government also encouraged women to join the Women's Land Army and the girls came from all classes, from London and the industrial cities, as well as from the country where women were used to muck and milking. Some were employed in gangs by the C.W.A.E.C. (County War Agricultural Executive Committees) and sometimes worked for eight months at a stretch on the threshing machines; not helpful for complexions or painted finger nails. Some of the girls were employed as rat catchers and two in their teens caught 20,000 in 18 months in the Welsh borders. Their uniform was green jerseys, brown breeches with brown felt slouch hats and khaki overcoats. Some of the ladylike women were shocked at the language which was usual among the male workers, but soon grew accustomed to the use of the word 'bugger' which most of the time was used as a term of endearment such as 'Blondie's got a beautiful pair of buggers ant 'er', or ''er be a beautiful bugger bent 'er?' The girls would turn their hands to anything within reason and one was supposed to have cleared the field at a ploughing match, beating all-comers, though I would like to know how she turned a heavy plough. Of course, it could have been a light one-furrowed plough on light soil.

The British farmer was seriously at war from 1939 as farming had been put on a war footing in the previous spring, and the first plough-up achieved its target by April 1940, and for every acre of ground or grassland which was ploughed up during the following winter the farmer received a subsidy of £2. Because of the importation of cheap corn from the New World many farmers had let good arable land go to waste. Drains and ditches had been neglected and hedges were allowed to grow to a width of more than ten yards, in some cases providing a good home for rabbits to burrow and breed. In almost every part of the country there were large tracts of derelict, overgrown land where bracken, gorse and briars had usurped fertile ground. Now the farmers ploughed seven days a week despite the freezing weather, sometimes at night with boys walking in the furrows ahead of the horses, where there were no tractors, with lanterns, unless the moon was shining. To carry a lamp or use tractor lights permission had to be obtained from the A.R.P. (Air Raid Precautions) authorities.

The Ministry of Food was always screaming for more potatoes saying that one acre of arable crops fed far more human beings than one acre of grassland, whilst one acre of average wheat saved at least as much shipping space as seven acres of the best grassland in England. And the best grass in England was not immune, not even the lush grazing land of Herefordshire with its rich red loam soil, the best in the country!

In the orchards of Kent, Cambridge and the West Country, farmers ploughed between the trees; the flower growers of Devon and Cornwall planted potatoes and carrots instead of their bulbs; the Great Park at Windsor was turned into the largest wheatfield in the country, and the Sussex Downs was planted for the first time since the days of the Saxons in the fifth and sixth centuries. In fact every available inch of ground was planted with something or other and the C.W.A.E.C. told the farmers what to plant and how much they would be paid for their produce, and where to sell it.

One farmer was shot because he didn't want to plant a few acres he had been ordered to; he was told to quit his farm, but barricaded himself into the house. The police were sent to throw him out, but he shot at them with his double-barrelled shot gun, wounding several policemen; the police broke into the farmhouse and the farmer, still putting up a fight, was shot down. He was acclaimed as a martyr to civil liberty by the Farmer's Rights Association.

There were also corrupt officials in the C.W.A.E.C. which was mostly made up of farmers. In one case a tenant farmer was evicted in favour of his landlord's son-in-law and in another case a farm was taken over by the brother of a committee member, reminiscent of goings-on with which I later became familiar in South America.

In 1939 there were over half a million farm horses and most of the work was done by four-legged horse power; a lovely sight to behold and environmentally preferable to the noisy, stinking, tractors with their excruciating racket on the roads today. Uncle Bert didn't buy a tractor until 1941 so that he managed with his shires and a wagoner who could be anyone available. Edwin, the second son, had volunteered to join an artillery regiment, the Shropshire Yeomanry, at an early stage of the war, which left brothers John and George and my brother Stephen, roughly aged 23, 17 and 16 respectively, to do most of the heavy work on the farm. John and George's sister Rose was still at school, studying the piano and doing the office work for her father. I understand that Steve, unlike his clot of a brother, was mechanically minded, as well as his cousins of course, which is essential with machinery on the farm otherwise progress is held up whilst the tractors are away waiting to be attended to by the mechanics. Unlike a lot of farms in the country, Monnington Court Farm had not been neglected because of the disgraceful Government's policy, and was in good nick. As uncle had forty or fifty dairy cows, plus followers to provide for as well as a flock of sheep, he was no stranger to cultivating the land for root crops and corn. There was no bracken, briars or bushes to be uprooted and destroyed when the campaign for food production began.

Prior to uncle taking over Monnington Court Farm, he farmed near the Welsh border and had a milk round in the market town of Hay-on-Wye, which he began at the behest of a couple of Welsh ladies to whom he was trying to sell a couple of rabbits he had snared the previous night. In their lilting Welsh voices they had said 'Why is it you don't try to sell some milk in town, man, we could do with some competition like?' On his return home he discussed the idea with Aunt Alice who was sympathetic to the proposal, and the following Wednesday on market day in Hay he paid £150 for ten friesian cows, and walked them home. That was during the 1920s farming depression. Around the time that Uncle Bert moved to Monnington Court, the Milk Marketing Board was established through which he got his outlet with Cadbury's of Leominster.

My father was then a sprightly 47 years of age and rose early all the year round in all weathers, to make sure that the cows were milked and the milk ready to be collected when the lorry called. Although I had spent some time with my family and relatives I didn't see much of my Father, as no sooner had he had his supper than he was off up the stairs to commune with his beloved Lord Jesus Christ, and retire for the night after a heavy day's work. I suppose we had not very much in common for we hardly spoke two words. The ten days leave of absence having gone like lightning, it was time for me to return to my unit.

It has been suggested that some of the boys after their experiences at Dunkirk forgot to return to their battalions, but as far as I am concerned that is pure nonsense. I have been given to understand that the men's families waited at the stations with a suitcase of civvies so that they could make a quick change and vanish. Where to, and what would they live on without a ration book? Who would employ them without an identity card which was necessary during the war? The suggestion is a load of rubbish.

Nevertheless, 6,000 people who could afford the passage and had relatives in the States arranged to join them, whilst the rest of the population were determined to remain and defend their country.

The official scheme for evacuating children was abandoned after 2,955 had been sent out of the country, but private evacuation was permitted and the blue bloods and wealthy queued up at Southampton docks with their children in their Rolls Royces and Bentleys, with stacks of baggage to last them for the rest of their lives. Some recent politicians who spent the war years in the U.S.A. had the gall and temerity to expound their views on the loyalty we owe to Crown and Country. They had abandoned the ship and it wasn't even sinking. They were to live in the lap of luxury while the rest of the population faced Hitler's bombers.

8
The Years of Suspense

We were sent from Aldershot to Wakefield where we spent two weeks in 'civvy' billets living a civilised life with delightful Yorkshire families. Meanwhile, the process began of reforming the battalion which had been somewhat reduced in numbers as a result of having suffered several casualties. I don't think the actual number was known until we had formed up on the playing fields of Wakefield and reported our names and numbers.

After our fortnight's further recuperation we were moved again, south-east across country to the charming little market town of Louth in Lincolnshire and were billeted in and around the area. Our immediate task was to patrol the coast in our newly provided bullet-proof 15 cwt trucks, keeping a lookout for German para-troops that were expected at any moment, the most likely possibility being an hour or so before daylight, the time they landed when they overwhelmed the Dutch. However, Hitler's barges were being heavily bombed as they were being prepared for the invasion and he couldn't make up his mind about what he considered to be a dangerous move. We remained on our toes for the rest of what turned out to be a cushy number, taking time off to attend the dances held in Louth's town hall, where we were able to meet some of the charming young ladies of the locality. Quite a number of the chaps were so enthralled by the lassies of Louth, having got their feet under the tables, that they decided that it was where their future lay and tied the knot. Together with a friend of mine at the time (though I refuse to mention his name now as not long ago, after a 45 year gap, I phoned him up to be told it was a long time ago and it wasn't worth renewing old acquaintances), I met a couple of girls who were in fact sisters, who used to take us home for tea and wads after the dance. With mother safely in bed we used to turn the sitting room lights off and snuggle up together on separate couches, each side of the room, with a couple of yards between us. There were some strange noises emanating from that room!

Because of the shortage of cash, my old friend Bing Yeomans, who is long dead and gone, suggested that we should take up professional boxing as they held professional matches in Grimsby, a few miles away by train. He decided he was going to be my trainer and manager and organise the fights. Thinking that the army would never find out, I boxed under the name of Jackie Brown and fought the same man three times as he was the only opposition available. The matches were bouts of six rounds apiece and we were so well matched that he won one, I won one and we drew the third. There was always a woman at the ringside shouting 'come on Jackie' and one night she invited me to go for a 'drink'. But I had to refuse because my 'manager' and two seconds were waiting for their fish and chips which was the ritual after each fight, plus a couple of pints to wash it down. Even after all that expense I was still left with a few bob out of the £5 I was paid for the fight.

My professional career came to an abrupt end when one day I ventured forth into town and came face to face with our beloved R.S.M., not a very polite Regimental Sergeant Major at any time, whose beady eyes noticed that one of my overcoat buttons was undone. He told me to report to the Guardroom where the Sergeant of the Guard was to 'put me in the book for being slovenly dressed.' The following morning I reported to the Orderly Room, whence I was marched before the Commanding Officer where the R.S.M. stated my crime as follows. 'Sah, on the morning of the 26 January [my birthday] I found this man walking about the town of Louth improperly dressed.'

The C.O. 'What do you mean Sergeant Major, he was walking about with his flies undone?'

R.S.M. 'No Sah, not as bad as that Sah, I should have said slovenly dressed, Sah. He'd one of his overcoat buttons undone, Sah, and looked a frightful mess, Sah, walking about the streets.'

C.O. 'How disgraceful, Jay, you ought to be ashamed of yourself after all the time you've been in the Guards.'

Me. 'Yes Sir, I am Sir, I'll be more careful next time, Sir. I am very sorry Sir'.

C.O. 'Right Jay, 10 days confined to barracks and 30 days deprived of all privileges, and be careful in future.'

Me. 'Yes Sir, thank you Sir.'

C.O. 'Right, march him out R.S.M. at the double.'

'Sah.' R.S.M. to me 'Right turn, double quick march, left right, left right, left right, left right, halt. Stand at ease.' R.S.M. sends for an escort to Guardroom. Escort arrives, R.S.M. to escort 'Take this idle man to his billet and form up with him, one in front and the other behind.'.

Escort Corporal. 'Attention, quick march,' and then they leave me in the billet to my own devices. During this time I was available for all fatigues, such as spud bashing and washing floors and all the usual parades, but not allowed to go out at night unless it was on guard.

On completion of my punishment I was transferred to another part of the county with the transport again. One day, when everybody else was on some sort of parade or looking for Germans, I had been left behind to keep watch on the billet and having not much to do decided I'd go for a spin on a motor-bike that had been left in one of the sheds. I had never ridden one before, but I got it started and off we went faster than was intended. I got round the first bend safely enough, but by the time we got to the second we were out of control and I was not quick-witted enough to reduce the speed. With tremendous effort I succeeded in turning the corner only to find myself in the ditch with a fractured clavicle and leaning against the bank. If it had not been for the good fortune of there being a house in the vicinity, I would have died from exposure as it was impossible for me to move. But the good people heard something unusual and came out to investigate which resulted in my being lifted out of the ditch, thanks be to God, and helped into their house where they gave me a cup of tea and called for an ambulance. I was still only 20 years of age and, as I've said before and will say again, was inconsiderate and thoughtless, because any normal human being would have gone back and thanked those lovely people for having helped me, but not me.

I was taken to the General Hospital in Louth where I was laid on a bed with a sandbag between my shoulder blades, and left there for a week forbidden to move. The nurse was asked how it would be possible to use the bedpan if not being able to move and she replied 'just lift your backside up with your legs, but don't move your shoulders.' It actually worked. After being in that position for a week I was allowed to sit up, during which time my collar bone had knitted, though it remained not a pretty sight for the rest of my life and has stuck out like a spare bone. After ten days I was discharged from the hospital where I received the best of attention, and although the faces are rather blurred after 51 years, there remains a picture of the bed and ward where I was so admirably cared for. God bless the nurses of Louth.

Even in those days there were 'joy riders' but on this occasion fortunately the only person who was injured was the 'joy rider' himself. It's a miracle he didn't break his stupid neck. It only occurred to me recently that the Company Commander must have taken compassion on me and considered that I had been punished enough for my misdemeanour, because I was not 'put in the book'—put on a charge—for taking the motor-bike without permission and marched before the C.O. to be sent down for a couple of weeks, but instead was transferred from the transport section once again. This time for longer than I care to remember.

My professional boxing career was further jeopardised now that I had broken my collar bone, because although it had set there was an ugly protrusion which, if it had been constantly played on by an observant opponent, could have come apart. So for the time being returning to the ring was out of the question.

There were other sports in which I could participate, however, and one of them was my favourite. With someone I had met in town with whom there was an immediate rapport, I decided to go to London for a week, to see the sights and old stamping ground with the official blessing of the powers that were; that is to say during a week's furlough. I should have gone home to see my parents, but the attraction of that certain something of the opposite sex was too overwhelming for me to resist the temptation of the tryst. What fascinated me more than anything about Elena was her beautiful auburn hair that hung down to her waist and a bit further! On a soldier's wages one can hardly say we hit the town and painted it red, but what with one thing and the other, mainly the other, we had a rip-roaring time, and with Elena bright-eyed and bushy-tailed I just managed to crawl back into my billet and bed.

Soon afterwards, in the spring of 1941, we were again on the move, this time to Paisley, near Glasgow, and for a short while we camped there pending a trip abroad, so we learned later, which never materialised. Whilst there we gave a concert for the local inhabitants. By this time I had developed quite a repertoire, including 'The Russian Rose', one of Monte Rey's favourites, 'Marialena', and 'Perfidia' others of his and 'O sole Mio' which wasn't. With the usual accompanist, Roger Wright, and a few more of the boys with their mouth organs and Timber Wood with his bath act impersonating a lady having a bath, we held forth in the local Social Club. One or two of the locals joined in and altogether we had a jolly good do. The ladies of the Club Committee gave us a slap-up supper at the end of the performance.

Headquarter's Company Sergeant Major who organised the 'do' sent for me and, wondering what I had done wrong this time, I reported to him 'at the double' but was relieved to find that I was to accompany him to the Club where a young lady wanted to meet me, as she thought I'd got a good voice. But the attraction did not extend further and I'm afraid that she was somewhat disappointed in other respects. The friendship never developed into anything other than platonic, but you can't win them all can you?

From there we moved to Castle Douglas in Kirkudbrightshire and believe it or not the battalion became short of drivers again. I was put back on the transport. One of my favourite jobs, on which I remained thanks to my old boxing 'manager' Bing Yeomans, was to drive him to the butcher's to collect the battalion's meat supply. As I was driving the truck Bing would be slicing off a couple of juicy steaks for our supper later in the day when we returned to our Nissen Hut by Carlingwark Loch where Bing, having borrowed a frying pan from the cook-house, prepared our sumptuous steaks on the solid fuel stove in the middle of the room. The rest of the boys would be lying on their beds slavering at the mouth, which was an extremely embarrassing situation for me, but for Bing, who, was an N.C.O with the exalted rank of lance corporal, it was revelry itself; a riotous feast and he was completely oblivious to the rest of the troops starving to death whilst languishing on their beds.

Some time after we moved to Kirkudbrightshire I got another ten days' leave, but this time I went home as it was likely that I wouldn't get another chance for some time as we could have been going abroad. But as I was passing through 'the smoke' I though I'd visit some old friends near Gray's Inn Road whose son-in-law was in the regiment. No sooner had I arrived than we had an air raid and this was during the time when the doodle-bugs were falling. Not being far from King's Cross Tube Station the folks picked up their bedding and rushed helter-skelter for the Tube, the best shelter in the area. Tubes as shelters were officially rejected by the authorities, but the public over-ruled them and bought platform tickets for a penny halfpenny and camped on the platforms. Sometimes the attacks would last all night and on this occasion it lasted well into the morning. People couldn't kip down properly until the trains had stopped running at about midnight, and until then they'd be singing and dancing on the platform accompanied by somebody playing an accordion. There were no toilet facilities so that you would have to wait for the trains to stop running before you could go up the line for a hi-diddle-diddle. Tubes could be dangerous and there were some terrible accidents. One station was hit in which 600 people were taking shelter; at another over 100 shelterers were killed; and at a third a small bomb scored a direct hit and the splinters from the tiles on the walls killed 30 people.

Many were made homeless due to unexploded bombs (U.X.Bs.) because all premises had to be evacuated and at one time there were thousands of U.X.Bs. waiting for treatment. One which landed near St Paul's Cathedral was removed to some marshes by the Royal Marines and was exploded; it left a crater of 100 feet in diameter. Buckingham Palace was hit three times during the blitz and the Queen said 'I feel we can look the East End in the face now.' On the 15 October there were 410 raiders over London and 400 civilians were killed, with 1,000 injured. The Café de Paris was hit in March when it was full of young officers on leave. Snake Hips Johnson's band was playing and they were all killed. People looted the watches and rings off the dead.

Early in the blitz people re-discovered the existence of a fine set of caves in the hills at Chislehurst in Kent. Families commandeered a cave and made their home in it, furnishing it with beds, tables and chairs and a chamber pot (!) because there were no toilet facilities. If they wanted to do anything else they had to do the same as in Pakistan and India—go out into the bush. They carried the water from a nearby stream and used lanterns with kerosene or home-made lamps with a bit of four by two. Special trains from London were run every night and the caves eventually came to have their own barber's shop, concerts and church services. Several thousand people dwelt in the caves in complete safety.

The most abominable shelter in London was found under the Tilbury railway arches in Stepney. People from all over London converged on it, often numbering 14 to 16,000 a night with no sanitation. If people wanted to do their business they just walked a short distance away and squatted in full view of the multitude. Being the East End of London it was a very cosmopolitan community and everybody mucked in; there was none of this business with 'what's yours is ours and what's mine is my own.' There was a war on and no class distinction. Prostitutes used to take their clients there during the raids and have it off in some quiet corner, unmolested. The shelter became the eighth wonder of the world and spivs would charge tourists for sightseeing. American journalists who were taken there threw up at the mere sight of conditions, but most of the people enjoyed themselves singing and dancing where they could find a clean space.

Boys used to take their girl friends to the empty, as they were dangerous places to be, dress circles in the cinema, whilst certain public shelters were monopolised by courting couples. Everybody became fatalistic and argued that if your number was on it the bomb would get you. Even Churchill said 'when my time is due it will come.' There was a saying in London that the Germans had developed a bomb that chased you round corners.

On 18 June, 1944, the Guards Chapel, near Wellington Barracks, was hit by a flying bomb whilst a service was taking place, and 119 people were killed, including many distinguished officers, and over 100 seriously injured. It has since been rebuilt and is one of the show pieces of the capital definitely worth a visit.

Having survived the night by spending it in King's Cross Tube Station, I proceeded to the safety of the Herefordshire countryside and spent a quiet week at home with my parents, seeing little of my father as usual, as for him it was work, eat, prayer and sleep, but I managed a fleeting glance now and again.

Returning to Castle Douglas in Scotland we were miles away from the bombers and the war going on over London and other parts of the country. We continued to have our dances in the town hall and I met a beautiful little girl who, like Maurice Chevalier's song, 'had a wonderful little nose, a wonderful little chin and wonderful little feet, in fact she had everything wonderful, you know!' After she had agreed to marry me I went to see her father to ask his permission, and he said 'Ye better ask her mother, she's the boss.' As a chauvinist all my life this was rather off-putting, but nevertheless I ventured forth, not knowing quite what to expect, and when I asked for her daughter's hand she said, in her Scotch voice, 'When ye ha' a job of work ye can, d' ye ken?'

'Yes madam,' I replied, and crept back to my beloved where we had been having a cuddle on the carpet in the sitting room. But it was the last time I saw the lass—we were moved to Perth and our letters mysteriously went astray. Nearly 50 years later, after I'd appeared in the *Daily Express*'s commemoration of Dunkirk, she rang to apologise for the letter she had written, in which she probably called me the biggest bastard on the earth, but I had not received it, or any other, and she had not received mine either. I was anticipating that she was going to sue me for breach of promise, but when she told me that she had been happily married for 40 years I breathed a sigh of relief and promised her that 'I'll call round one of these days, *Deus volente.*'

Whilst we were stationed in what had been a Polish camp we were engaged in manoeuvres in preparation for the invasion of some far off land. We did not have the vaguest idea where that would be, as not even the most senior officers had much idea, although there were some wild guesses. On one occasion we went to Inverary where we simulated an invasion aided by the Navy, which involved climbing the face of towering cliffs without the aid of ropes. However, we were never called upon to climb any further rocks at any time, but the exercise did us no harm.

In those days we had not the capacity to go tearing about the country, as the pay did not cover more than a few pints and some fish and chips, not like today when members of the services drive their own cars, so we had to pursue our enjoyment in the area in which we were stationed. One night I was detained by an over-passionate young lady who insisted that I should stay to keep her company 'until her friend returned home,' which resulted in me being late for roll call the following morning. Who should be the Sergeant on duty, but my very good friend Matty Hayes, the south-paw of No Mans Land fame who admitted later that he only booked me for being absent without leave because he was full of envy.

As per usual I was marched up before the C.O. who, after the charge had been read out, said 'Anything to say, Jay?'

'Leave to speak Sir' says I—you always have to ask for leave to speak when you are on a charge—'I had spent most of the night on the bog because of an upset stomach and must have been there when the Sergeant called the roll. I'm sorry, Sir, that I wasn't feeling well.'

To which Lt. Col. Heber Percy, remarked to Drill Sergeant Baker, 'There must be some conflict in this case Drill Sergeant, case dismissed!'

Drill Sergeant Baker: 'Yes Sah.' To me, screaming at the top of his voice: 'Guardsman Jay r.....ight turn, quick march, left right, left right, left right, halt! Stand a.....t ease. Dismiss!'

9
North Africa

I doubt very much we knew where we were when we had arrived at the port, and certainly had not the remotest idea that we were about to embark for North Africa. But after nine days of the worst journey I have ever endured in my life, we arrived at Algiers on the 22 November, my sister's birthday, and I'd forgot to send her a card. We had had problems with the U-boats, having to turn back more than once and for most of us it was a matter of who could get to the ship's rail first, as we were all slithering and sliding about in our own vomit. I've never felt so ill in all my life and was jolly glad to see land. We disembarked and marched ten miles to the edge of Algiers, where we camped for the next ten days whilst awaiting transport to take us up to the front. During this time, if we wanted to go sight-seeing in Algiers we were obliged to thumb a lift or take a ride on shank's pony. Needless to say we stayed in camp most of the time, but a friend and myself did pay the town a visit once, with only one thought in mind, and that was to look over the talent. Being an Arab country this was somewhat difficult as they were covered from head to toe, including the yashmak they wore to cover their faces. Being in a strange country we ventured no further than the streets of the casbah, and certainly had no intention of entering into a mysterious establishment, in the doorway of which stood a tall Arab lady with only her eyes showing above the yashmak. Curious to see what she looked like underneath I pulled the yashmak to one side. She did not object or stand back, but glared at me with coal black eyes which prompted me to run away as fast as my legs could carry me, for fear of reprisals or a knife in the back. On reflection it was not a wise move. We returned to our bivouacs not much the wiser.

Finally our transport arrived, from the R.A.S.C., as our own was still having problems with U-boats and had been delayed. It would be three days before we reached our destination, having to cover about 600 miles, which meant bivouacking overnight along the way where we were fed and watered. One night I stupidly hung my lovely army greatcoat on a tree next to the tent and all I found for it next morning were five eggs at the foot of the olive tree. The nights can be cold and when on night duty you need something more than your uniform. It was some time before I was issued with another coat, as there were no spares in the stores.

At the time I was still officially on the transport, but without, as I have said, a vehicle. This proved to be a great inconvenience as my good friend, Major John Nelson, sent a message from the front to say that he wanted Jay, who was now an N.C.O. with the powerful rank of lance corporal—they must have run short of experienced and qualified men—'as he has had extensive experience on patrols in France.' 'Oh, bloody hell' thought I, 'you've had your chips this time mate.' So taking my leave of the lucky buggers waiting for their trucks I proceeded towards the sounds of warfare coming from the direction of Medjez-el-Bab, which became one of the many battle honours of the Grenadiers, (more precisely Grenadier Hill and number 3 Company). On the way I passed somebody who had copped it from a stray artillery shell; not a very pleasant omen, and joined the Company in the hills where we remained, more or less, for the next six months. Number one priority was to dig a trench which proved somewhat difficult as we were positioned on rocky ground, so all one could do was to scratch the surface and build a sanger with stones which would help to protect you from the shells and stray bullets. Apart from the nightly patrols this became our living quarters through all weathers and unfortunately at a time when we had frequent heavy rain storms. Not very pleasant to wake up soaked to the skin and no means of being able to dry our clothes.

Our primary task was to go out on reconnaissance patrol to try and learn the position and strength of the enemy. This was done when it was pitch dark, when you couldn't see your hand in front of you as on moonlit nights you would have been visible to the enemy. The hills were strewn with boulders so that we would have to creep about like cats, being careful not to fall over them and making a noise which would alert the Hun. One night, when it was lighter than usual, we came across what looked like a lot of men lying motionless on the ground, so as not to disturb them we quietly turned round and went home. I was shaking in my shoes and I'm sure the platoon officer did the right thing—if they weren't boulders it could have resulted in a nasty mess in close combat and it looked as though we would have been outnumbered.

I don't think it was due to any outstanding initiative or brilliance on my part, merely because they were short of a L/Sgt, but I was promoted to that exalted rank and the second-in-command of my section was a Jew whose name I wish I could remember. Soon after the traumatic experience of being promoted to L/Sgt we were detailed for what was to become the most dramatic experience of my life. The idea was that we had to move to a position overlooking Longstop Hill, another famous point on the map since the Tunisian campaign, with the object in mind of capturing a German. This could only be achieved at night or early morning. Our platoon, led by our platoon officer, Lt William Dugdale, L/Sgt Virgo—a fellow section leader, and another Sergeant whose name escapes me, together with our three sections totalling roughly 30 men, including three Corporals, were chosen for this special mission. When the plan of operation was spelt out to us it accelerated the not so dormant adrenaline. By 5 a.m. we were to reach a certain position and wait for the 25 pounders of the artillery to put down a barrage for ten minutes, after which time we would wait for 30 seconds and then proceed to where we considered the Germans to be in position. One of the sections, led by the Sergeant whose name I can't recall, would remain in a rear position from which to cover us, and Virgo and myself, together with our platoon officer and men, climbed the hill on which Jerry was entrenched. The platoon officer was on my immediate right and glancing to my right I saw the silhouette of a human being on the sky-line, and pointed this out to the officer who immediately turned right, at which point the enemy began firing at us. We immediately hit the ground until they stopped firing, and then we rushed the post which turned out to be manned by two men with a machine-gun on a fixed line, which was the reason they had fired at us with a rifle from the side of the sanger as we approached it from the north. They had obviously run out of ammo which is why they stopped firing. All we were armed with was a rifle and bayonet.

However, what happened next still fills me with amazement and incredulity almost to the point that one is led to suspect that there might have been a conspiracy to get rid of me, except that I had not been a Sergeant long enough for whom anyone had built up so much hatred. The platoon officer and the rest of the party grabbed one of the Germans and left me alone to cope with the other. I have lived with this for nigh on 50 years and I still can't get over it. Someone said that it was due to the quick thinking of the officer that we achieved our objective. There is no doubt that they were quick witted in getting away as fast as they could and following the officer, but all I needed was one or two men to give me a hand and we could have had two prisoners instead of one. Fortunately the one they left for me to handle was a short man about 5 foot nothing, but by this time it was beginning to look like Piccadilly with verey lights and flares going up all round us and some obvious activity in the surrounding enemy sangers and the position was becoming desperate with me trying to knock the little bloke out with the butt of my rifle, so that I could throw him over my shoulder and carry him home. I tried kind persuasion by saying to him 'Kommen Sie mit mich meinen kleinen freund, otherwise you're going to get a sore tummy', but all he kept repeating was 'nein, nein, nein.' He was completely unarmed because they'd only had one rifle between them and it had fallen on the ground in the sanger, so he tried to wrench mine out of my hands and finally grabbed the end of it and fell to the ground with my bayonet only half an inch from his stomach. It was a case now of it being him or me and it definitely was not to be the latter, even though I could have been surrounded by his mates at any moment—but they were probably shitting themselves as well. So there was only one thing for me to do and that was to deal with him and sling my hook as fast as my legs could carry me, without a glance to the rear, hoping I was going in the right direction downhill and over the wall.

It had been very dark when we arrived, but dawn was now beginning to break and after about half a mile I caught up with the rest of the platoon waiting for me behind a hill. The officer didn't say 'where's the prisoner then?', but he did want to know what had happened to him, and so did the Company Commander when we reported back to Headquarters.

On another occasion we were detailed to go out during the day and try to learn the position of the enemy. Lt W. Dugdale, Jack Nicholls, Harry's the V.C's. brother, and myself were to be the scouts, and there was a platoon led by a Sergeant, whose name no one seems to remember, or doesn't want to, who were supposed to cover us. We hadn't gone more than 500 yards before we soon discovered where Jerry was. He was up on Longstop Hill with a commanding view of the valley and wadis up which we were walking in broad daylight like silly buggers waiting to be shot. We were brought up sharp in our tracks when machine-gun bullets began peppering the ground within six feet of where we were walking, followed by the echoing of the heavy machine-gun's boom boom boom. The Great Architect had his eye on us once again; we were far too close together and should have been at least ten yards apart, but we dived into a wadi, a rocky watercourse dry except in the rainy season, and the lieutenant and Jack went one way and I went the other, just to be awkward. The Germans were by now shelling the area, hoping the shells would drop into the wadi, but they were, by the Grace of God, falling on each side of the gully, but more or less in line where I was walking. Fortunately, it turned out the wadi was horseshoe-shaped and led us back to our company position. Suddenly, to my consternation, as I turned the corner I came upon a lot of abandoned weapons, a red fez which some stupid bugger had been wearing and a lot of empty sardine tins; the platoon had been having their lunch instead of watching out for us; they were supposed to have been protecting us, but instead the sods were having a picnic and had been taken prisoner in the process because they'd not even had a 'look-out' on duty. A wadi is very deep, but it is possible to find a position where you can put your head above the parapet, as it were, to watch for the approaching enemy. Both enemy attacks had been co-ordinated so that when the Hun had been firing at us, his raiding party had come over the hill 50 yards away, creeping like cats, to intercept our covering platoon on which they had swooped whilst they were busily having their sardines and hard tack. I had not heard a sound, but it transpired that they had shot L/Cpl Blank who had been wearing the fez—the Jerries obviously thought he was an Arab collaborating with us, which is why he was shot first. The rest being taken unawares no doubt threw up their hands and surrendered and were taken prisoner. L/Cpl Blank died in a Tunis hospital and is buried in the Medjez el Bab War Cemetery. C.Q.M.S. (Basher) Burton, another of our old friends, who has long gone over to the other side, gave me a lot of this information when I emerged from the wadi. He had watched everything taking place from his Observation Post but, of course, was helpless to do anything about it. He could hardly have called for an artillery barrage. This unfortunate incident took place at the beginning of March 1943.

The end of the Tunisian campaign came on the 12 May when the Germans 'threw in the towel'; they not only threw in the towel, but everything they could lay their hands on was going up in surrender; white sheets, shirts, handkerchiefs and dirty underwear were being waved, admitting defeat.

My Company Commander suggested that I should call on some volunteers: you, you and you! No, for once it wasn't like that at all, they all did volunteer and ten of us with orders to 'go and find the Germans' climbed the hill in arrowhead formation, as big head suggested—me—and on reaching the summit crawling on our knees so as not to expose ourselves, discovered the Jerries in the valley below nonchalantly standing around laughing and joking, and having a smoke, chuffed that for them the war was over and they were still alive. To bring them to their senses I ordered the bren-gunner to fire over their heads, to which they responded by waving anything that resembled a white flag. As we were going down the hill, a snotty-nosed sergeant who should have been leading a section of men, but instead was driving it, shouted out to me, 'I'm senior to you, I'll have this lot.'

To which I bellowed back, 'Bollocks, why don't you piss off, you snivelling little creeper, they surrendered to us, not you,' and we proceeded to relieve the prisoners of their weapons, including an Italian berreta which fitted nicely into the palm of my hand and which I kept for myself. I later sold it for 500,000 lira, about £5, in Naples when, as usual, short of readies. We then marched the prisoners back to our Company Commander and handed them over for safe keeping.

From then on it was plain sailing and all we had to do was round up thousands, perhaps 250,000, prisoners who were standing around in groups, discussing their future—in which country they would spend the rest of the war and what the girls would be like were uppermost in their thoughts. After all they were young men like ourselves, most of them having been taken out of school. The area we rounded them up was the Cap Bon Peninsula where the Germans were hoping to be picked up by boat to transport them back to Sicily and Italy, but they missed it and instead of drinking chianti they'd be lucky if they got a glass of water. We marched them to prisoner-of-war camps in Sousse, where so many people today spend their holidays, and where we were to guard them for the next two and a half months from mid-May to the end of July. During this time we were able to take it easy and loll about on the beach, as well as celebrate our delayed 1942 Christmas dinner which our Commanding Officer had promised 'when you have thrown the krauts out of Tunisia and North Africa.'

The population of Sousse at that time was in the region of 49,000, but it is understood that there were only two 'bints' in town who were at all inclined to 'socialise' with the troops and as a consequence they were kept busy 24 hours a day.

When the P.O.Ws. had been sent away we were first moved to Guelma and then to Constantine in Algeria where Matty Hayes and myself were ordered to set up the Sergeants' Mess and Corporals'

Mess respectively. This was a completely new line of business, at least for me, and involved making our acquaintance with the local wine trade which was mostly in the hands of French colonists. One of them had a beautiful daughter, but every time I tried to chat her up her old man would shout 'Allez-vous, tout de suite, s'il vous plait.' In those days it was difficult to get within speaking distance let alone touching.

My friends such as Bing Yeomans and others arranged a boxing match and matched me with the Algerian light-heavyweight champion of North Africa, and we did some training with an Italian prisoner-of-war who happened to have been a professional boxer in Rome. With several other bouts the fight was staged in the grounds of Constantine Hospital. The Algerian was a short, stocky, squat little fellow but powerfully built. He had somehow or other contrived to cover his gloves with resin and by the end of the first round my face looked like a skinned tomato. Nevertheless, with a straight left punch to the nose and a straight right to the jaw in rapid succession, which I had been practicing with the Italian, he was counted out in the second round. Looking the mess I was, I was advised to go to the hospital for some treatment and the lovely little nurse who belonged to the Queen Alexandra Nursing staff with their red, white and grey uniform, suggested that it would be better if my whole face was bandaged completely, and did a magnificent job.

The highlight of our sojourn in Constantine was a concert which the Sports and Entertainments Officer had the brilliant idea of staging for the Brigade in the enormous theatre in the centre of the town. Through intelligence we discovered that there was a famous French opera singer living in Constantine, and with her we organised a scene from Rudolf Friml's and Herbert Stothart's 'Rose Marie' in which I was to sing the part of Jim. (It's a pity we hadn't got the Canadian Mounted Police choir in the background). There was no chorus accompaniment. The Sports and Entertainments Officer took me to Madame Duvetalalit's apartment and introduced me as the great lover to be. She was living in Constantine with her mother, I presume as an exile from German-occupied Paris, for rather than entertain them she preferred entertaining the Allies. Madame Duvetalalit could not speak a word of English and I knew not the music of Rose Marie, so she being an accomplished musician played the piano and taught me my part and I in turn coached her in the lyrics, probably sounding very much like a Herefordian with a sweed-basher's accent. Madame Duvetalalit, Duvet for short, was a short, round, little woman with breasts that stood out like two balloons, in her late 30s, very late. To a mere boy of 23 she was ancient, and although she floated on a cloud of Chanel she stank of garlic every time she opened her mouth; being a singer that was quite often. One thing she had in her favour was that she was a brilliant artist and you couldn't help being influenced by her personality. It was the first time I had been involved with anyone at such a high level and was quite nervous, which she sensed immediately and kept repeating that I should say to myself 'Je suis calm' as often as possible.

My French was also limited but with a lot of miming from the professora and gentle persuasion we forged ahead in our pursuit for perfection, and after a number of rehearsals in Madame Duvet's apartment, with never ever a cup of coffee, we were ready for the big night.

Of course, we were not the only ones taking part; there were the usual turns such as Timber Wood and his impersonation, the mouth organ band of which we possessed the best in the Brigade, an accordion player, a comedian and a crooner, but we were what is termed 'top of the bill' and came on almost at the end of the concert. Roger White was the pianist as usual as there was no way we could drum up an orchestra in the town.

Our contribution was Rose Marie's and Jim's duet, the 'Indian Love Call' and after one bar of four beats, Rose Marie comes in with 'Ooh ......' for two and a half beats and then after one and a half, Jim, who is off stage imitating Rose Marie, echoes her call, after which Rose Marie sings her solo:-

So echoes of sweet love notes gently fall,
Through the forest stillness,
As fond waiting Indian lovers call,

When the lone lagoon, stirs in the spring,
Welcoming home some swany white wing;
When the maiden moon, riding the sky,
Gathers her star eyed dream children nigh,
That is the time of the moon and the year,
When love dreams to Indian maidens appear.
And this is the song they hear:

When I'm calling you --- oo-oo-oo-oo-oo,
Will you answer too --- oo-oo-oo-oo-oo,
That means I offer my love to you,
To be your own,
If you refuse me, I will be blue and waiting all alone;
But if when you hear my love call ringing clear,
And I hear your answering echo, so dear,
Then I know our love will come true, our love will come true,
You'll belong to me, I'll belong to you.

Then the duet comes in for encore, repeating the above.

Jim walks on to the stage as the great lover and holds Rose Marie in his arms, but in this case it was not possible to get too near her as her balloons got in the way and at the end, instead of Rose Marie putting her head on Jim's shoulder she put it on his chest and he rested his chin on the top of her head because of the 12" difference in height. As a final gesture Jim kisses Rose Marie on the right cheek and to do this he almost had to get down on his knees and then swoops her up in his arms and carries her off stage, but unfortunately not into the boudoir. There was no after dinner celebration as I remember and we were lucky if we got a cup or mug of sprog — tea — before going to bed, but I can still remember the occasion after 48 years. It would be interesting to know what happened to Madame Duvetalalit.

A month or so later we received orders to embark once more, for a secret destination.

10
Cassino, Italy 1944

On 2 February 1944, after a delightful break from combat activity for a period of eight months, we sailed from Bizerta in North Africa, to Naples in Italy.

Having got a bit browned off with my roll as 'a patrol specialist'—not my words but the Company Commander's—and having experienced some close encounters, I wormed my way back on to the transport section by having a word with the Transport Officer, Lt (Katie) Meyrick who was fortunately short of staff.

One of my first jobs was to drive the Company Commander to the Officer's Club in Naples for dinner, and whilst waiting for him to return I had an unforgettable view of Vesuvius erupting with the red balls of fire rolling down the hill. The volcano is slightly southeast of Naples and the red lava looked quite menacing.

Our battalion occupied Cassino in March 1944 and moved into the cellars of the town which lay in ruins after weeks of shelling and where we lived for two weeks at a time with 25 or 30 men to the remains of a house. There were no toilet facilities as the sewers had been destroyed by the bombardment, so that if one wanted to defecate, shave or shampoo, one would have to seek the shelter of a wall or rubble facing south and be accompanied by two bodyguards as look-outs for Jerry snipers as they would be tempted to shoot it off. The men lived, cooked on their tommy-cookers, had their meals and slept in the holes, and no one went sight-seeing as there was no need for patrols. It was just a matter of watching and waiting.

Hoping for a cushy job on the transport I found we probably had the most dangerous one, carrying ammunition, food, water and fuel up Route Six, the main highway north to the troops in the Cassino fox-holes. The fields on either side of the road were flooded with water and the roads and bridges had become impassable as a result of the bombardment by the Germans in their retreat, so that everything had to be manhandled nightly in ruck-sacks over the destroyed bridges, past bombed-out buildings, abandoned vehicles and bloated dead bodies lying about in the water. The moonlit nights were the most dangerous as we could easily be picked out by the snipers as we found our way through the ruins, and on such occasions our artillery would put down a barrage of smoke-shells into the German sector. It has been said that accompanying the sounds of the artillery there would be the sounds of frogs and nightingales to help us on our way, but I'm afraid I did not hear the nightingales. I wish I had.

One night when I was passing the food and ammunition down to the blokes in the cellar, I saw a Jerry out of the corner of my eye throw something through the doorway which landed on the floor with a thud. About 20 years later it occurred to me what it might have been — a grenade which failed to go off thanks to a saboteur, one of Hitler's slaves working in an ammunition factory, who probably saved my life.

Our transport was parked in some olive groves about 8 kilometres behind Cassino and word filtered down that my cousin Edwin was up front with the Shropshire Yeomanry Artillery Regiment and I was allowed to go up front to find him, which was a pleasant surprise. When I caught up with him, as Sergeant he was laying the law down to his crew and firing at the Germans. When they had finished he walked back with me to the olive grove, until we were shelled in response to Edwin's bombardment, having to take cover in a nearby gully until the shelling ceased, after which we returned to our respective positions.

After the costly action in attempting to storm Monte Cassino in which 80,000 allied soldiers lost their lives, the flower of youth, it was decided on May 11, 1944, to launch an encircling offensive across the Rapido and Garigliano rivers. This opened in the early hours with a bombardment of hundreds of guns in the Liri Valley but without attacking Cassino itself, and after one of the fiercest battles lasting six days, Cassino was virtually cut off. Behind the natural obstacles of the two rivers the Germans had erected formidable defensive positions, but not as impregnable as Monte Cassino. Our troops were still in position in the ruins of Cassino and were able to witness the Jerries running up the mountain, dashing from one rock to another to dodge the shells and bullets in their attempt to get away before being intercepted and surrounded. When dawn broke our boys were faced with an abandoned town of rubble and rotting corpses, mostly German. They had won but at a great cost.

Another concurrent battle was taking place further up the road at Anzio, which had turned into a disaster due to the incompetence of the American Corps Commander, Major General John P. Lucas, simply because he had decided to wait for the tanks instead of pushing ahead to Rome which the scouts had reached unopposed. Whilst Lucas was consolidating his position the German commander, Kesselring, decided to attack, almost driving the 50,000 Anglo-American force back into the sea. Of our 5th Battalion Grenadier Guards, nine officers were killed, ten wounded and nine taken prisoner. Of the other ranks 52 were killed, 222 wounded and 30 missing, most of them being taken prisoner. Major General Lucas was replaced, needless to say, by another American, Major General Lucius K. Truscott, a much younger man and a much wiser tactician. I'm too old now to be considered for a medal or to be even 'mentioned in dispatches', so I can say without the possibility of being sentenced to jankers and spud peeling, that one of the things I resent most is for young men in the prime of life having to lose it because of someone's incapacity to see further than the end of his nose, especially when a Government has spent a fortune on training the officer to lead them.

Several weeks later and much farther north, but south of the Gothic Line which the Germans had built 'beyond which no allied soldier would pass', Corporal Jimmy Coles and myself were delivering a tanker of water to the troops in the front line near Dicomano, just south-east of Florence, when a shell landed on the road a few yards ahead of us, which brought us up rather sharpish and left the boys up front short of water. I felt no pain, but my left leg and right arm went stiff and I said to Jim 'Bloody hell Jim, I've been hit,' and the water truck stopped of its own accord. Jim was perfectly all right, miraculously enough, and organised transport for me to be taken back to the Advance Dressing Station which had been set up in a church hall, with beds laid out as in a hospital ward (the army has an incredible organisational ability and it took tremendously good care of its wounded). Lt Meyrick came to see me and jokingly said 'You want to hurry up and get better because the troops are getting thirsty and haven't got any water with which to make their tea', but he knew that I'd be—hopefully for me—out of action for some time. Feeling sorry for myself as Mr Meyrick was disappearing through the door, I shouted out 'Will you please write to my Father and Mother and tell them that I've been wounded.' He said he would, but ever since I've thought what a little baby he must have considered me to be having only suffered comparatively minor injuries. Two pieces of shrapnel had gone through my arm near the elbow and had come out on the inside, and several pieces had lodged in the back of my leg. There was no reason to have worried my parents, and I don't suppose the Lieutenant wasted time in writing to them; he had more important things to do, like finding a driver to take the water up front.

From the dressing station I was taken within a very short time to a hospital where I was operated on, and before being put to sleep, and not having seen my leg, I said to the surgeon 'I'm not going to lose the leg am I doctor?' To which he replied, 'Don't be so bloody silly, you've only got a bit of shrapnel in it,' and then I got the needle and woke up the following day in a South African hospital in Florence looking into the blue eyes of a beautiful blonde-haired Boer descendent. But that's all you could do, look, because they were all officers and wouldn't allow you to do anything else unless you'd got at least one pip, though they preferred captains or majors.

I spent Christmas 1944 in the South African hospital and was flown in an Air Ambulance to Naples to spend the New Year in another hospital where I remained for two weeks. (Didn't I say the army looked after its troops?) From there I was sent to a South African convalescent camp where I remained for another three weeks having the time of my life. The camp was near Caserta, roughly 20 kilometres from Naples which cost about 50 lira to reach on the bus, the equivalent of a shilling. One of the first things I did—no, you're wrong—was to go and find a singing teacher as I knew the Italians were the best in the world. El mio Italiano was nil at the time, but I managed to find a maestro who gave me a few lessons and said there was something wrong with my voice production and asked why I couldn't relax. I quipped that I'd been in the Grenadier Guards too long and you never relaxed in the Grenadiers, to which he replied 'You'll never be able to sing if you don't relax'.

It wasn't until many years later whilst at the Trinity College of Music that I was told what I was doing wrong. However, I continued doing whatever it was that was wrong and entertained the troops convalescing in the camp. The South African sergeant-major came round asking everybody if they could do a turn as he was organising a camp concert, so I, being always keen to oblige, volunteered to sing a couple of songs. Thinking I was Richard Tauber I began making gestures with my hands during rehearsals, but the sergeant-major said that Richard Tauber never did anything like that. 'If you are a solo singer you keep your hands by your sides and don't move about.'

It has been said that after a few muscatels in Naples I used to stand on the tables to serenade the signorinas. Friggy Friar used to accompany me on the accordion, another of our old friends who's probably playing a harp now, as he passed away some time ago.

All too soon I was returned to my battalion. I'm afraid I am not like someone who said he'd got fed up with being in the hospital and defying doctor's orders had returned to the front line as he was afraid of missing the action. He was missing it all right. The C.O. who had taken over from him had been killed and he couldn't wait to go the same way by the sound of it.

No sooner had I rejoined my unit than I was wounded once again. This time I had got a lift on the back of a motorbike ridden by a drunken red cap—military policeman—who took the wrong turning and drove towards the front line instead of away from it. He drove into a zone being shelled by the Germans, one of the shells landing on the road in front of us knocking us both off the bike, the red cap being wounded in the left arm and me with a badly wounded right leg, just missing the shin, but leaving a 5" gash to the right of it. The M.P. put a field dressing on my leg and one on his arm, then left me sitting on the side of the road and went in search of an ambulance as it was impossible for me to sit on the pillion. Although he was drunk the incident had brought the red cap to his senses and he was aware of his responsibility. Within half an hour he had returned with an ambulance, much to my great relief, as it had occurred to me that in his state he might have forgotten all about me.

I had brought this on myself, as I've brought many a disaster, as a consequence of being too fond of the opposite sex and on every occasion I had only myself to blame, no one else. A friend of mine who was in charge of the Officers' Mess, who'd got to go and do some shopping with a three-tonner, therefore invited me to accompany him to Perugia where he'd got a girl friend, and where he'd got to make his purchases. Strange as though it may seem, my friend's girlfriend, had a girlfriend who was keen to meet an English Tommy, especially as he was good looking (!) and in the Grenadier Guards. We spent the afternoon in the loft and fell deeply in lust and she wouldn't allow me to leave without her, saying she wanted to come to England with me after the war. I didn't particularly want to leave her either as she was a real Italian Venus, never having seen anything like her in my life; she was beautiful and and about 17 years of age my friend thought after I had explained the situation. 'If you want to get in the back it's all right with me', so I lifted Josefina up over the tail-board and we made love all the way home. 'Home' to Pontassieve which is due east of Florence and the nearest town to the front line where I could find accommodation for Josefina. I found a charming Italian lady who was prepared to provide a spotlessly clean little flatlet for my 'wife' for 15/- a week, which would leave me with about 15 for myself and the occasional loaf of bread for Josefina. 'La mia moglie' was very happy and couldn't wait for me to return, but for now I had to 'thumb' it to camp feeling quite chuffed with myself. The landlady promised that she would look after 'La mia moglie' and I paid her a week's rent in advance and promised to return on the following Sunday. But someone up there had other ideas and I was to be taught a severe lesson. Instead of my being able to visit my true love I was blown up *en route* and landed up again in Florence, in the same hospital, gazing into the same beautiful blue eyes of the blonde-haired Boer descendant, to whom I ventured, 'Fancy seeing you again. I'm sorry, but I couldn't keep away.' To which Staff responded with a cold steely look of contempt as much as to say 'how dare you speak to me, an officer in the South African Nursing Service.' I remained there for less than a week, which was just as well under the circumstances, before being flown by Air Ambulance to Naples. (What an expense a wayward rascal can cause). Being in a British hospital, a military hospital, is almost like being back in barracks as it's run on the same system and discipline, which is what one would expect. After two weeks of exceptional care and attention I was discharged to the South African convalescent depot for two weeks, and this time I took advantage of the rest to visit Pompeii.

There was also an opportunity to visit the San Carlos Opera House in Naples, where I had the privilege of hearing the great tenor of the day, Beniamino Gigli, sing in La Traviata. I thenceforth determined that I was going to be an opera singer, but I was already 25 and had had only three lessons from my Italian singing teacher in Naples. Little did I realise that to be any kind of singer, besides having a voice you needed to be a musician, and to get the right sort of training you are best advised to join a church choir at the age of 9 or 10. Unfortunately I have never had my feet firmly planted on the ground being the romantic, fantasising type. Only at 72 am I beginning to settle down!

By the time it could be arranged for me to re-join the battalion it was in Austria, and on 8 May the war in Europe was over. Eventually I joined my unit on the Klagenfurt Lake in Austria and there discovered that the lorry driver had been 'looking after' Josefina. He apparently had been there like a shot as soon as he heard that I was out of the way and in Naples, but in a way I was relieved to know that she had been taken care of, as the situation for me proved to be quite hopeless. There was absolutely no way I could have kept in touch with her.

We remained in Austria for only two weeks, but during that time I met an Austrian fraulein, much against the rules and regulations as we were not supposed to fraternise, but nevertheless arranged furtive appointments in the pine woods some distance from the camp. Elsa could speak a little English, but apart from a few words like 'ich liebe dich', 'biteschöne' and 'kommen Sie mit mich meinen kleinen freund', my German vocabulary was somewhat limited and no matter how many times I said 'ich liebe dich, biteschöne' she wouldn't sit down under the trees, so all we did for ten encounters was to walk about the woods holding hands. She would say 'nein, I want to come to work in England mit you and then ve will get married and sit down anywhere you like.' She knew vot she wanted to do, nein? I explained to her that my Commanding Officer might not want her to come to England with me as there might not be room on the boat—we were supposed to be going to Naples to catch a ship. She replied by saying 'never mind, you can send me the money for the fare and I will make my own arrangements, but first we must get engaged before you leave Austria.'

Elsa had lovely blonde hair, typically Austrian, with all the curves and bumps in the right places, but not frightfully good looking, quite mediocre really and nothing to write home about, but quite sure of herself. She'd only got one thing in the forefront of her mind and that was her determination to go to England, and I only had one thing on my mind which wasn't to go to England for the time being. I promised to send her the money if we could find a compromise, but I wasn't prepared to get engaged and certainly wasn't in the position to make a down payment on the fare which was another condition she specified. I've never been what is termed today, streetwise, but I began to think she was something of a con artist. Maybe she wasn't and sincerely wanted to go to England, though it was no better than peaceful rural Austria surrounded as we were by the lovely pine woods and the lake. Food was scarce, but it was rationed in Great Britain as was everything else, including clothes. So we continued to hold hands and walk in the forest under the pine trees, hidden from view of the beady eyes, regrettably not being able to even sit down, until we were torn apart, thankfully— let us end this painful torture—by another move, this time to Fano beyond Rimini, Pesero and Ancona, on the Adriatic coast where we camped in bivouacs for at least two months.

Someone had worked us a flanker. It has been said that my battalion, the 3rd, of which I had been a member since 1936, had amalgamated with the 5th in March 1945 and that the privileged favoured veterans from the 3rd had returned on a troop ship from Naples bound for Blighty to be inspected by our Colonel, Princess Elizabeth, at Wellington Barracks in London. However, those such as myself who were also veterans and who had been 'in it up to our necks' since the outbreak had not had our names called out, were condemned to remain in Italy to soak up the sun, sea, sand and sex! A lot of things happen in the army that you know nothing about until after the event.

I don't even remember being able to kiss Elsa good-bye, not on the lips anyway—she was determined to protect everything she'd got and was very jealous of it! I wished her better luck next time and hoped that she would have a prosperous future. I have no doubt that she made a success of her life.

It was said at the time that we were also programmed to leave on a troop ship from Naples, but were later informed that a cholera epidemic had broken out. That may have been an excuse for the delay, but nevertheless it meant that we had to wait for the brass to make arrangements for our transport and this was going to take time as there were many thousands of men to go home.

There was literally nothing for us to do on the beach at Fano except twiddle our thumbs, swim and cavort. We had not had the opportunity to do much sight-seeing and there wasn't much to do in Fano as it was only a small town with a population of about 20,000 souls who had never been farther than the back door, so we had not a great deal in common. Some of the inhabitants, out of curiosity more than anything else, came to see what we were doing camping on the outskirts of their town, not making it too obvious by just walking along the beach accompanied by some of the local talent who were mostly well chaperoned and not allowed to linger. I had erected my bivouac not far from the beach so I had a panoramic view of the procession. However, that was all we were permitted for the time being apart from the odd stray who would brazenly take a dip in full view of the troops.

Not long after we'd arrived at Fano we decided to organise a trip to San Marino, a small republic of 61 square kilometres and roughly 90 kilometres from Fano. We more or less 'commandeered' a municipal bus for the day and rounded up a load of squaddies to pay the republic a visit and have a meal and a few drinks. San Marino is the capital of the republic with the same name and lies 23 kilometres south-east of Rimini on the eastern border of the Apennines. At 745 metres, Monte Titano is the highest of its three peaks, on each of which is built a castle. The republic attracts large numbers of tourists with the sole purpose of admiring the picturesque old houses and streets, as well as the magnificent views from the republic. We were able to over indulge ourselves with heaps of spaghetti bolognaise and litres of chianti before returning to our bivouacs in complete control of ourselves, except for the odd song or two, which is the wont of troops no matter where they are. Our favourites included 'Roll out the Barrel', 'It's a long way to Tipperary', 'You are my Sunshine', John Brown's body lies amouldering', and 'There's a Tavern in the Town'.

The following day we were back to normal; one of the signorinas I had noticed came sauntering along the beach on her own, stripped off her clothes to reveal a posh one piece bathing costume—Italians didn't wear bikinis in 1945 and I don't think anyone else did either—and flung herself into the brine. This was just before mid-day and it was almost time for tiffin, but hold your horses, Bernardo. Gloriana didn't stay too long in the water as she said it was 'troppo freddo'—too cold—and came to lay on her towel on the beach about 20 metres from my bivouac where I had been admiring the scenery. As 'a faint heart never won fair lady, la la la la ...', I ventured forth with 'Buon giorno, signorina, come sta, lei?'

'Benissima, grazie; e lei?'

'Io sto bennisimo, grazie signorina?' So far so good. I sat down on the beach beside her and stared at the sea with one eye and at her luscious figure with the other. 'Come si chiama, lei, signorina?'

'Mi chiamo, Gloriana, e lei?'

'Mi chiamo, Bernardo, signorina.'

'Molto bene, ho appetito.' It was past time for lunch, so I asked her to excuse me.

My friend Steve was on duty in the field kitchen and as I had done him a favour in Austria by doing a disappearing act in a moment of crisis, with a whisper in his ear my mess tins were over-flowing—the large compartment with a generous portion of pork chops, potatoes and peas and the smaller compartment with peaches and custard for duff, and a nice big mug of sprog—hoping that Gloriana would still be there when I returned, as I'd heard they would do anything for a tin of sardines! She was, but now preparing to go home. However, I managed to persuade her to stay for a bite which wasn't difficult when she saw the amount of food I'd brought especially for her.

'Piaciere mangiare?'

'Per favore, non molto.' So she ate all the sweet, but said she didn't want to eat much.'Grazie mille; non ho appetito.' When she had finished and drank most of my tea and said she was very sorry—'mi dispiace— and that she was now going home—'vado a casa.'

'Dove casa?'

'In citta,' she said, Fano.

I thought I'd chance my luck and asked if she was coming to 'my house' tomorrow and she replied 'non posso, domani,' she couldn't come tomorrow. Tough luck, Jay, try again another day.

'Arrivederci, signorina Gloriana.' Patience Jay, be patient. 'Ritornera presto'—come again soon.

We had the surprise of our lives when our Company Commander suggested that some of us could go to Rome for a week, as there wasn't much point in hanging around Fermo; there was still no news of our departure. Why could we not have gone to the north of Italy, through to France by train to Calais and ferry home, instead of hanging around in Fano? It would have been a lot cheaper than going by air which we eventually did. No importa, it was only at the tax-payer's expense of whom governments spend millions, like the French on the Maginot Line!

The more fortunate of us were issued with passes to spend a week in Rome to where we had to find our own transport. The distance was roughly 160 km across country and the easiest way was by bus, the only problem being that they were prehistoric and the tyres were like my head—bald and punctured easily. We left Fano before break of day and arrived in Rome, famished and thirsty, about midnight. Fortunately the driver knew where the services' hostel was so he dumped us in the street outside. We pinned our passes upon the lockers at the end of our beds so that they would be visible to all and sundry, but as usual the red caps paid us visits at regular intervals making a nuisance of themselves, and causing us great inconvenience even though our passes, our permission to be on leave, were staring them in the face. So we thought 'bugger this mate, let's go and find some company', which did not prove too difficult in la citta di Roma, and they weren't men needless to say. Reg and I found two bella signorinas who volunteered to take us in for a few days and to show us the sights! Mine was an artist, though I never discovered what sort of art she practiced, as she would always leave me outside the 'theatre' and I had to kill time for a couple of hours every evening until she had finished whatever she was doing!

During the day we managed to persuade them to take us to see St Peter's and the square where the Pope makes his speeches. Both the church and the square are enormous and the Piazza di San Pietro (St Peter's Square) is a veritable masterpiece by Bernini the artist— a different kind of artist—which took 11 years to finish. The square can accommodate nearly half a million souls and is surrounded by 140 statues of saints. Five of Italy's greatest architects died whilst working on St Peter's, including Michelangelo who, in 1546 was forced by Pope Paul III to take on the job of completing the building. People in casual dress are not allowed entrance to St Peter's or the Vatican Museums. Women aren't allowed to expose their shoulders and arms above the elbows. Mine even wore a hat. The fifteenth century bronze doors have been saved from the old basilica, the original. Michelangelo's statue of the Virgin Mary holding the dead body of Christ on her lap in the chapel is the only one that he ever signed. Michelangelo was afraid that someone else might get the credit for the sculpture so he crept back one night and signed it on the left of the Virgin's clothing.

You can climb the stairs from the entrance to the roof of the church. It's a difficult climb and the stairs are steep and narrow, and one way only so you've got to keep going. When you reach the top you are rewarded with fantastic views of Rome and the Vatican gardens. The Pope holds mass audiences on Wednesday mornings, but we missed him. You have to get up early to be there by 11 a.m.

On another day we visited the Colosseum, one of the most famous buildings in the world. Gina the artist, 'la mia bella ragazza'—my beautiful girl—knew quite a lot of people, especially men and was always greeted by someone or other with 'buon giorno' and 'come sta lei? bella ragazza e que cosa fare lei questa sera?'—'what was she going to do this evening', and she would always reply 'lavorare naturalmente'—'work, of course', 'sempre lavorare'—always to work. Gina was obviously very popular and always provided a good service! She was also always hungry and as she was the boss off we would go to a spaghetti house for 'un piatto di pasta y un bottiglia di chianti' which was the cheapest meal you could get in Rome and probably still is if you go to Piazza Risorgimento where there is a simple trattoria with a long name La Mejo Pastasciutta der Monno. Everybody knows the Italians are very fond of spaghetti and why not, it's good and cheap. It only cost 100,000 lira (10/-) for the two of us. Inflation was rampant in those days and that was after the Allies had burnt billions of lira. (Incidentally, talking about pasta reminds me of a meal on the way up through Italy where I persuaded the cook, Steve, to provide an Italian lady with some flour so that she could make us some spaghetti a la Italiana, and for sweet she gave us walnuts. Her husband had made a 200 litre barrel of wine, so we had plenty to drink. He was a prisoner-of-war in South Africa. 'Buon salute, Antonio.' We drank his health several times.)

When we had dined Gina had to rush off to the 'theatre' so she would kiss me on the lips and tell me to 'aspettare due ora.' I'd got to wait for her for two hours twiddling my thumbs and drinking another bottiglia di vino. I wouldn't be much good for anything except sleep by the time she'd finished work, so I would find a cosy little trattoria and sit outside on a chair near a table watching the crowds walk by. It was always the same trattoria so that Gina knew where to find me, and then we'd have a night cap and saunter home to her apartment. She wouldn't allow alcohol to be taken into the apartment, she said it deadened the senses and gave the wrong impression.

One evening we discovered Irving Berlin was going to give a talk and recital especially for the troops stationed in and around Rome. Even in 1945 Irving Berlin was a famous composer of light music and the theatre was packed with standing room only. He was dressed in his First World War uniform with putties up to his knees and a long officer's jacket over his breeches, and talked of his early life in Russia and emigration to the USA. He was unable to write or read music himself, but played the tunes running through his head on the black notes of the piano whilst a musician friend would write down what he heard. His first great hit was 'Alexander's Ragtime Band' which made him famous, and in 1922 he had a theatre built which was known as the Music Box for the purpose of showing off his compositions. In the 1930s Fred Astaire sang his songs such as 'Top Hat' and 'Cheek to Cheek'. He also wrote the music for 'Follow the Fleet' in which Fred Astaire and Ginger Rogers starred. One of his greatest hits was, and still is, 'God Bless America', another Easter Parade', yet another 'White Christmas' and 'There's no Business like Show Business' from Annie Get Your Gun. It was a memorable evening and I can still see him standing on the stage in his dark green uniform.

Reg's girlfriend had taken the night off to visit a friend, sex undefined, since she was not interested in coming to the show and didn't know Irving Berlin from Adam anyway. After a couple of drinks we went our separate ways heading for our respective lodgings and 'bella ragazzas'. Mine was waiting for me on the door-step and filled with incandescent rage like Vesuvius with lava dripping from her lips and a torrent of Italian swear words which were incomprehensible to me, but they helped Gina to get a load off her mind. As she kept repeating 'altra signorina' I understood that she thought that I had been with another girl and I tried to tell her that I'd been with Reg to see Irving Berlin, but of course she had no idea who he was so didn't believe me. Finally she pulled me upstairs by my hair and threw me on the bed where we made it up just to prove that I had not been with another 'ragazza'. After this experience I was loath to mention that we were due to return to Fano the following day, as I was afraid that she might take drastic steps to prevent me from leaving like locking me in the apartment while I was asleep. So I waited until I had taken her to the 'theatre' the following evening before explaining that I had to leave to catch a boat with the regiment the next day and that we were travelling over-night to Fano. It naturally came as a bit of a shock, but as we were standing outside the theatre there was little she could do about it and I gave her a handful of 10,000 lira notes, with which she was more than satisfied, and kissed her good-bye. I'm sorry to say that I was filled with a great sense of relief after the experience of the previous evening and most of the night which had left me shattered.

Some women are insatiable. We actually returned to the shelter and cloak of the services' hostel for another two days, but kept well away from our stomping ground and from possessive females with abnormal sensibility to enjoy a few days in which to recuperate before returning to Fano to the sun, sea, sand and ...

At the time there was only one way to travel across country without making too many changes and that was by bus, but this time we had a good scout around for a not too prehistoric omnibus with good tyres. We decided to make an early start in the morning with a bus leaving at 4.30 a.m. With a smoke screen put down by the vehicle and the sound of heavy machine-gun fire issuing from the exhaust we took off at 6.30 a.m. after some difficulty in getting the engine started. It broke down on the outskirts of Rome. Telephones were almost non-existent and if you found one it didn't work, so the driver thumbed a lift back to the main garage where he achieved the miracle of being provided with another bus. It was mid-day before he arrived with the replacement, but we happily transferred to our new bus, by this time not caring too much about the delay as we'd bought a couple of bottles of red wine and were merrily having a sing-song with a few of the boys going the same way. The tyres were not in such good condition but the engine proved more reliable, except that it needed topping up with oil every 30 kms. The driver carried a 50 litre drum of oil in the boot. We had to change at Spoleta, but with the delay we had missed our connection and had to stay in a spotless pension for the night in a room with half a dozen Italians of various ages.

The following morning we embarked on a similar old banger, but this time the journey back to Fano was uneventful and we arrived just in time for Italian bangers and mash, with bread pudding and white sauce and our usual lovely mug of sprog. My bivouac was still in place, my next door neighbour having kept his eye on it, and now it was my turn to look after his. For the next few days we took advantage of the magnificent weather to swim in the Adriatic and although there were other girls accompanying their elders, Gloriana did not appear, much to my disappointment. She obviously had no intention of tasting the forbidden fruit. She only liked peaches!

Not knowing the length of our stay in Fano I decided to make inquiries in Ancona, roughly 32 km to the north, for a singing teacher as there wasn't one in Fano, and was directed to the College of Music. The college wasn't prepared to help as I could give them no specific duration for studying, but they did send me to a maestro di canto whose wife aroused him from his siesta and over indulgence of the bottle, and who appeared in his dressing gown explaining that he'd had 'molto mangiare e troppo vino rosso.' He wasn't terribly keen to waste time on someone who was here today and gone tomorrow, but because everybody was short of money il maestro condescended to give me some lessons. For the next hour we were going up and down the scale with him playing the piano.

It was the first and last time I saw him, because the following week we were on a train for Bari and a flight home on a Liberator with no seats. We just sat on the floor of the plane. We arrived in England in no time and landed at Peterborough airport from where we were sent to Hawick in Scotland, where we lived in Nissen huts for the next few months. Because I had done a bit of boxing they made me sports' storeman and I had a lovely Nissen hut all to myself.

Having been abroad for nearly three years without being able to get home to see our parents, we were given ten days furlough to visit the family. No doubt my parents thanked the Lord for my safe return, but not a word was uttered to me. They were not the demonstrative type like some who would throw their arms round you and say: 'How wonderful to seeeee you darling dearest son! It's been aaaaages ...' They probably said: 'Oh you're home then? Did you have a nice journey? When are you going back?' Dad, as usual got on with his milking and praying and was most likely very pleased that the war had ended, but continued to live in his private world, never showing any interest in what I'd been doing for the last three years. Neither did anyone else for that matter.

When I returned to Hawick I had an audition with Carol Levis of Carol Levis Discoveries thinking I was going to take the country by storm, but no sooner had I opened my mouth than he said 'That's enough' and called for the next contestant. So much for Britain's next Enrico Caruso! I should have taken the hint, but I battled on regardless.

Whilst we were stationed at Hawick they held the Scottish boxing championships in Edinburgh and a few of us entered the fray. I had developed a middle-aged spread by now even though I was only 25, and had to move up to the heavyweight class which was a disadvantage to me when meeting heavier opponents. It was my last fight, though no disgrace. The other man had come charging at me like a bull and I gave him my secret combination, the old one two, straight left and a right to the jaw which left him swaying like a tree in the wind, collapsing on the ropes when the bell saved him. Next time he came out of his corner with his guard up and got me in a corner and caught me with the lace of his glove on my right eye causing it to suddenly close. Fortunately, the referee was on the ball and noticed what had happened, for you don't fight with one eye. This was my last endeavour, as although the powers that were had invited me to return to the championships, considering that I had suffered an unfortunate mishap I gave them the excuse that I was out of shape and not fit enough to take part. My plans lay elsewhere.

Nicholas Farmhouse, Winforton, where I was born on January 27, 1920

The Sun Inn, Winforton, in 1997

Top left: L/Cpl W. 'Matty' Hayes, later Sgt. 3rd Battalion Grenadier Guards
Top right: Guardsman Harry Nichols, later awarded the VC
in Belgium, 1940
Bottom: Recruit W. 'Matty' Hayes and his squad at Caterham Depot in 1937.
Matty is fifth from right in the middle row

Top: King George VI inspecting our Battalion,
the 3rd Grenadier Guards, at Perth in 1940
Bottom: Lord Wentworth, No 2 Company Commander and I believe a
descendant of the original commander of the Grenadiers, leading his
troops back from Aldershot to Windsor

Sgt. Frank Dowling's Squad at Caterham Depot, 1936. I am seated on the extreme left of the front row

Recruit G. Webb and his squad at Caterham Depot in 1939. Webb is fifth from the right in the middle row

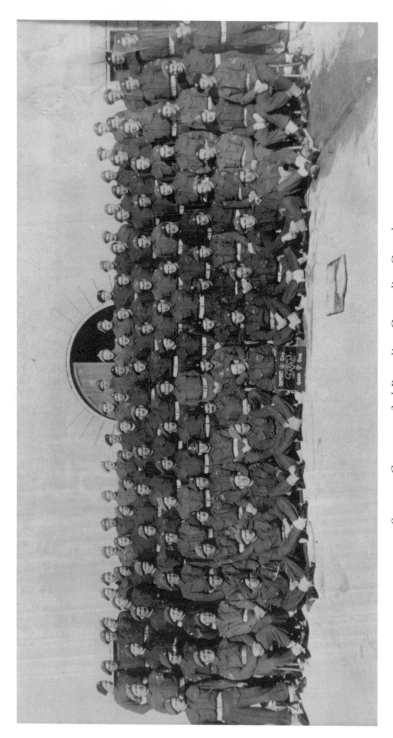

Support Company, 3rd Battalion Grenadier Guards

*Top: My old farm in Venezuela being levelled by
Alvaro Barbiero in 1991
Centre: Outside my old farmhouse when visiting Venezuela in 1991
Bottom: The lyceum in Acarigua where I taught English*

Top: My villa in the Algarve, where I lived from 1979 to 1985

Middle: My Nephew Neil Jay's sons on his farm in Wales

Bottom: Nephew Wendell Whittal-Williams' sow and piglets in Wales

11
Demobbed 1946 : Trinity College & the Hippodrome

We had by this time moved down to Amersham, prior to being demobbed. A friend of mine who thought he was doing me a great favour suggested to the Rehabilitation Officer that I might like to go to a college of music. When I was offered a place I couldn't believe my luck and jumped at the chance as I still considered that I had the making of a Gigli at least, if not a Caruso. When you are young and immature, which I have always been, you never face reality and are forever fantasising. On reflection, with all the experience I'd had in agriculture, I should have tried for an agricultural college where I might have been set up for life. But now my mind was made up, especially as someone else had had some faith in me to have suggested going to a college, even though at 26 I didn't know a crotchet from a quaver. A singer's life is short-lived in comparison with that of a farmer, who seldom retires unless he's made pots of money and even then he keeps his beady eye on his off-spring. The obvious road to have taken would have been that of an agricultural student, but it is now water under the bridge. I had an audition with Sir Granville Bantock, President of the Trinity College of Music, London, and sang for him the old chestnut, 'Take thou this Rose'. It must have sounded dreadful to someone who might have preferred Handel's 'Waft her Angels to the Skies', but it sufficed to get me into the college. Returning to Amersham to be demobbed, I was given a chit to collect my new blue pin-striped suit from the Army's outfitting centre in my home town of Hereford and spent the summer picking fruit on a local fruit farm before the new term began at college.

After ten years in the service of His Majesty and the country, it was somewhat difficult to settle down at college with a lot of people with whom I had little in common. There were only a handful of ex-servicemen and women, and they were on refresher courses in the field of teaching having already had a thorough grounding in their chosen profession. I, as a complete learner, felt right out of my depth. Most of the students were in their teens and had spent the war years in the wilds of Wales as evacuees, had always been in school in one form or another, and were all miles ahead in the theory of music and its appreciation.

Ivor Warren was my regular singing teacher and because I had developed a bad singing habit, he sent me to a colleague of his to detect the problem and discovered that I had been singing with the larynx in the back of my mouth instead of relaxing the bottom of my throat. It became quite a problem trying to sing and pressing down on the larynx at the same time. However, Ivor Warren's colleague whose full time job was singing in the choir of St Paul's Cathedral helped solve the problem. If one has a voice one should be encouraged to join a choir, or choirs, school and church, where a child would get the finest musical education. Another priority is being able to sight read from the musical score, something that I could never do. The Welsh use the tonic solfa notation even for singing hymns from the cradle. I can't even sing a third or a fifth even to this day, unless I play it first on the piano, but I can't pitch them.

Apart from voice training we had to cover theory of music and music appreciation, which were not my favourite subjects I'm afraid, and I chose to learn to play the piano (no wonder a girl friend's father suggested that I should be at work with a pick and shovel) as a second subject, which I thought rather more appropriate than a trombone, for instance. At least by learning to play the piano one can bang out a tune with one finger if you know what the notes are, but to co-ordinate the left hand with the right was beyond me, although in the army I just about managed to co-ordinate my right arm with my left leg when marching to guard Buckingham Palace. Needless to say, I did not make much progress with the piano, but at the age of 72 I now have a bit of fun on the organ trying to play hymns.

Anxious to get a foot in, I was given the opportunity to audition for the B.B.C. through a friend, who knew a friend, who knew a friend, and made a record in Wigmore Street at an agency, but it did not impress. I also had an audition for 'Bless the Bride' with C.B. Cochran and out of the eight who were auditioned, two of us were invited to sing again, but the other bloke pipped me at the post; I cracked on the last note and was shaking like a leaf. A friend knew a friend who was producing a play in which someone had to sing a song, but I wasn't good enough. Jack Hylton was putting on a show at the Hippodrome, later to become 'The Talk of the Town', called 'High Button Shoes', and I auditioned for that as one of the eight male singers of the chorus and this time was accepted. The storyline was based on life in the United States of America prior to the First World War, notably around the Model 'T' Ford and the Ladies' Bird Watching Society.

There were an equal number of female singers who thought they were the cat's whiskers and were too good for us mere male morons. They probably all had Stage Door Johnnies as there were lovely looking ladies of tender years. We rehearsed in the basement of the Hippodrome for about six weeks before it was tried out at the New Theatre in Oxford with great success. If it had been taken on tour it might have lasted longer, but as it was it only ran for six months at the Hippodrome. One of the reasons was probably because the leading comedy man was an American unknown to the British public by the name of Eric Parker. Sidney James of later television fame was a singer/dancer in the show, but was unknown at the time. One of the ballet chorus members was Audrey Hepburn. She must have been no more than 18 or 19 at the time but even then was a very articulate young lady. She told a group of us standing in the doorway of the theatre how she escaped with her family from

Holland whilst the Germans were invading the country, had crossed Belgium and France with other refugees and, being more fortunate than most due to their diplomatic connections, were able to board a ship bound for Dover before the mass evacuation. Audrey, because of her nymph-like appearance, was soon whipped out of 'High Button Shoes' to appear as a statuesque clothes-horse in the corner of the stage at the Cambridge Theatre. Another of the chorus who made a name for herself was Alma Cogan. My nearest claim to fame was that I sang in the quartet that introduced and opened the show and did a sort of gig in the process.

I was still attending the Trinity College of Music where I remember having coffee with Amy Shuard and her accompanist Thelma Lawrence, both of whom were somewhat older than most students, although still only 22 years of age. Amy Shuard had been studying the piano from the age of three and so had a thorough grounding as a musician. She made a name for herself at the Royal Opera House, but unfortunately died when quite young so deprived the world of a superb soprano, though she remains unforgettable in the main part of Puccini's Turandot. Amy Shuard thought that I 'should go back to the farm'—she was not being unkind, just sensible and realistic. Another famous lady, Joan Cross, the internationally known soprano and one of the founders of the New English Opera Company, to whom a friend had introduced me and with whom I had several private lessons, thought that 'I should go and grow tomatoes.' She too could have saved me a lot of time if only I had listened to her. Apart from not having the necessary musical background the range of my voice was too limited as I was unable to reach a top 'C' as required by all tenors, some being able to sing top 'D', for which a Swedish tenor is famous. Having spent all of three years studying music and voice I think most people would want to obtain some benefit from it.

A theatrical agent fixed me up with a summer season in Swanage which lasted three months, and a pantomime in Derby of Robinson Crusoe with nobody of note, which lasted for the season. My main memory of the pantomime was that I suffered stomach trouble at the hands of the lady in the 'digs' who probably cooked in the same fat all the year round!

Most of the time, approaching six months of the year, unless you are an exceptionally good singer or have regular employment in a cathedral choir, you spend on the dole. If you are just very good you might be an understudy to one of the leads, or an understudy of an understudy! Alternatively, for anyone who wants to spend his or her life in a chorus, there are opera choruses which employ a certain number of singers. In 1963, during a singing competition in Hereford, an adjudicator suggested that I was a bass, this after spending almost three years studying as a tenor in Trinity College of Music. Quite frankly if I had my time over again I would, as many wonderful singers do in Wales, just join a choir and sing for the pleasure of it, and stay at home and milk the cows!

During this time I had met a young nurse who later became my wife. We had met whilst I was performing at the Hippodrome and she was staying with a friend and doing a mid-wifery course in the district. Not having seen her mother for three years, who was married to a Dane in Venezuela whom she'd met in Cuba during a voyage on a Cunard passenger ship, Jackie decided she must go to Venezuela. Immediately before she left on a ship from Southampton in the summer of 1949, she came to say good-bye and we spent a couple of hours together in my 'digs' in Swanage, where I was then singing. We knew she was pregnant, but she was determined to go to Venezuela whilst I was just as determined not to marry her if she was so intent on going, with no assurance that she would return. I was still intent on a future in the theatre in Great Britain, where I at least had got a foothold and an agent who obviously had some faith in me. Indeed I was rather pleased at the way things were progressing.

However, nearly twelve months later I had been persuaded by my future mother-in-law, whom I had not yet met, that my duty lay in Venezuela—she had sent me a photograph of my daughter—and I bought my passage on the 'Golfito' passenger/banana ship. It was whilst I was actually moving out of my flat at 3 Sinclair Road, West

Kensington, London, that I had a telephone call from my agent asking me if I'd like to go on tour and then to the West End with the 'White Horse Inn' as an understudy to John Hanson, the internationally known tenor. My first reaction was one of extreme disappointment as there was nothing I could do about it, having paid £100 for my trip to Trinidad and made all arrangements to leave the country. All I could say to my agent was that I was very disappointed at not being able to accept the offer as I was going abroad, and it was impossible to change my mind as everything had been arranged. I deeply regretted having to turn down the opportunity as I might have made it in operetta as there are few, if any, top 'C's' in the score. My heart sank to its lowest as this was the first great chance—providing that John Hanson went sick a few times during the tour! Perhaps he'd at least have caught a cold, or better still the flu. It was not necessarily the end of the world as Lil, my mother-in-law to be, had suggested that I'd have no problem getting on the radio over there. Little was I to know that that was to turn out to be 'pie in the sky'—the first essential if you want to sing in South America is to speak and sing in Spanish and have a repertoire of boleros.

Whilst I was waiting for the 'Golfito' to sail from Southampton I went back to the land, where I should have stayed, and drove a tractor for my brother Steve who was managing a farm for a Lady Mary in Wiltshire.

12
Venezuela

I had some difficulty in getting a visa from the Venezuelan Consulate in London. In 1950 the Venezuelan government had very strict control over immigration, particularly by people from Britain, despite the fact that Tamayo, the Minister of Agriculture, was in Europe encouraging people to emigrate to colonise an agricultural colony which the government was establishing in Venezuela's Portuguese state. After I had explained that I had a daughter in Venezuela, it was suggested that I should go to Trinidad, which was only 30 minutes by air to where I wanted to go. I was to buy a return ticket so that I could produce it at the Venezuelan Consulate in Port of Spain, Trinidad, allowing me to obtain a 14 day tourist visa. Having arrived in Venezuela I could then apply for an extension; first six months, then one year and so on.

In June 1950 I set sail for South America. My mother-in-law to be arranged for a friend of hers, a Senor Lopez from Puerto Rico who was living and working in Puerto de la Cruz, Venezuela, to meet me in Trinidad and accompany me to the Venezuelan Consulate. I'm sure that Lil just wanted to make sure that I arrived for she was the instigator of my move. It was she who had done all the writing and thought it was important for me to be there, like all the older generation would have considered it to be. Jackie hardly bothered to write. She was perfectly happy with the way things were. There were lots of young American males who were fancy free with good jobs as engineers working for the oil companies, and young European and American girls were thin on the ground.

People seldom consider what you are going to use for money when they make these arrangements for you. I had managed to scrape together the £100 by disposing of my piano which I had bought on the 'never never' whilst at Trinity—it had cost me £80—and cashing in an insurance policy, but all I had left was loose change. I stayed for a week at an inexpensive guest house, where the proprietor made you wear a jacket for dinner even in that heat, whilst arranging for my flight and visa with Senor Lopez who had met me on arrival. The voyage had taken ten days and was a luxury I shall never forget especially as 'the company' was most entertaining. It was rather different to the ten days spent dodging U-boats and being sick during the trip to Algiers.

Lopez left two days later for Puerto la Cruz and I a week afterwards on a plane from El Piarco, Trinidad's International Airport, to Maturin in the State of Monagas in north-east Venezuela. On arrival I was instructed by mother-in-law to hail a 'puesto', a taxi for four or five persons, heading in the direction of Punta de Mata where the Sinclair Oil Company had their camp out in the wilds. In fact one camp for the American executives and another for the Venezuelan employees. Jackie was employed as a nurse in the hospital and had a house in the Venezuelan camp. Communication was difficult if not impossible, as there were no red telephone kiosks dotted about the country, so that it was a case of arriving without notice, even if one's arrival is expected. The taxi driver knew exactly where the camp was as Sinclair was a well-known oil company and a major employer in the area. Finding the hospital was also no problem. 'No hay problema' said the taxi driver as there were signs for 'Hospital' everywhere, the word being the same in Spanish and English. After some unemotional preliminaries—you'd never have thought we hadn't seen one another for twelve months, but it was in the hospital and we had to exhibit a certain decorum—Jackie was allowed the rest of the day off. After all, her boyfriend had come all that way to see her and his daughter, and she'd got to take him to see the baby. Jackie paid the taxi driver and we walked to her home where Olimpia, Jackie's nurse maid, was looking after Carolyn, or

Carolina as Olimpia often used to call her. She was a lovely little girl about six months old, and I was glad I'd made the effort to come and see her.

Wasting no time we jumped on a plane the next day in the company's airport of Punta de Mata, all three of us, and flew to Caracas, or more precisely Maiquatia. Caracas was reached from there in about an hour and a half on what is now the old road, winding over the hills and which had been built by Juan Vincente Gomez (1908-1935), or rather the tyrant's political prisoners working in chains. We stayed at Hotel Maracaibo, whose proprietor was an old friend of John and Lil Hanson, my future-in-laws, and the next day we were declared man and wife in a registry office in El Silenzio Square, with Carolyn as our one and only bridesmaid! 'No hay problema' said the Registrar when Jackie explained that we had 'no testigos' — witnesses — but 'queremos casar por favor' — we want to get married please — and in two shakes of a lamb's tail we were, with babe in arms. We had spliced the main brace and I had travelled 6,000 miles to do it without the threat of a shot gun.

We celebrated with Pepe, the Cuban proprietor of Hotel Maracaibo, with 'cuba-libre' — rum and coca-cola — and a paella.

The following day Jackie and Carolyn returned to Punta de Mata because she was on duty at the hospital. There was no time for a honeymoon and I was to stay in Caracas to explore the possibilities of pursuing my career as a singer. As I quickly found, the first priority is to speak the language of the country, especially if you are an unknown artist. If I had been a Luciano Pavaroti it may have been different. A Panamanian who had befriended me tried to arrange an audition with Billo of Billo's Caracas Boys on Radio Caracas, at the time Venezuela's most popular orchestra, and we waited two weeks at the radio station for an audition which he had promised to give. We were there every day from 9 a.m. to 5 p.m. waiting for Billo to arrive, but he never turned up and probably had no intention. Venezuelans can never say no, but they'll get the message over in other ways when you've spent a lot of your time hanging about. I went to the Mario Night Club in Sabana Grande where the proprietor said I could sing to the char ladies one morning, but no one came to see me when I had finished. 'Como no, Uds, puede cantar' they had said—you can sing, of course—but they were obviously not impressed with someone singing in English. Never mind, the char ladies enjoyed it!

I also went to see 'Papillon' Henri Charriere, in Baruta, Caracas, the man who escaped from Devil's Island, who had the restaurant 'Mi Vaca y Yo'—My Cow and I. Whilst you are dining he allows a cow to walk through the dining area and which had been trained to make a mess on the floor. I sang for him but I was not quite his cup of tea. I suppose I was rather naive to imagine that I was going to be able to make a living in Venezuela as an entertainer, but that had been the impression I had been given by my mother-in-law.

I don't know how I managed to survive in Caracas for two weeks, as at the time it was probably the most expensive country in which to live. Having realised the hopelessness of the quest and running out of the necessary, there was only one thing to do and that was to return to Punta de Mata with my tail between my legs and look for a job.

Back in Punta de Mata I was given a job helping to take the inventory in the spare parts department and warehouse. This created much ill feeling as the Sinclair Oil Company, like all other foreign companies, were only allowed to employ 1% of foreign workers. Anyone who could read and write and add 2 and 2 could have done the job given to me. As there were many Venezuelans queuing up to be employed by the oil company, I was the least popular new recruit on the work force. When the inventory was completed I was transferred to the Abastos—Commissary—where I was even more despised, as one of the main jobs given to me by the manager, a Mr Wilson, was checking the customers to make sure they paid for what they were taking out of the grocery store. They sometimes had two full polythene bags in their hands and it was suspected that they only paid for one. Though this was never proved, I had the distasteful job of standing by the cashier's desk and checking them out, being more or less the unofficial security man. I always suspected that the

Venezuelan book-keeper working in the office suggested this to the manager just to make my position even more intolerable.

It wasn't long before my dear mother-in-law put in an appearance, something which was to become quite frequent. The first instruction I received was to 'stock up with the drinks', which consisted on a case of beer and bottles of vermouth and gin for cocktails before dinner. This was completely alien to my life-style and I hadn't foreseen what I was dropping myself into. What I should have said to Jackie's mother when she suggested that I should go to Venezuela, if I had shown some strength of character, was 'if you send Jackie back to England I will marry her as long as she stays here, but I'm not abandoning my career in England to take a chance in a country where I don't speak the language.' But I had been easily led into something that was not to my liking either at home or at work.

Jackie's mother used to turn up whenever there was a fiesta in the club. The Americans frequently had reasons for a barbecue in the club grounds, or a party in the American Social Club, and the Panamanian organist Edmundo Munoz was usually engaged to entertain. This at least gave me the opportunity to render a few songs. Unless Jackie was on duty the following day, she and her mother used to stay in the club until the early hours of the morning though, because I had to be at work at 7 a.m., I left earlier. It became increasingly embarrassing to hear the two of them singing 'Roll out the Barrell' at the tops of their voices as they came through the Creole camp waking the natives, most of whom had to get up early to go to work. It caused a certain amount of tension and I was accused of being intolerant. Jackie had some support from the hospital administrator's wife, whose husband I was to meet at a later date with his arms wrapped round a mestiza in Caracas.

As a result of taking part in the club's entertainment, I was often invited to sing in the surrounding social clubs, and it was frequently suggested that I should go to the States and try to get on the Ed Sullivan programme, which was then more or less the equivalent of the Carol Levis show in the U.K. My standard reply was 'Thanks a lot, but I've been through all that several times before.'

Secretly I persisted with my hopeless fantasy and envisioned myself performing on the stage at the Radio City Theatre in New York.

I shall never forgive myself for allowing a tremendous opportunity to slip through my fingers whilst I was working in the Commissary one day. A friend of ours, a Dane, who was employed as the Transport Manager for the Sinclair Oil Company exploration camp, came to the store and asked me if I knew anything about road building as the Company wanted somebody to supervise the building of a road in the State of Barinas on the other side of the country near the Columbian border. I didn't know anything about building a road but that, on reflection, shouldn't have presented much of a problem. All I had to do, because Bill Agaard already suspected that I might be interested otherwise he wouldn't have come to inquire, was to say no, but you can tell me what to do. I hadn't known him that long, but we had been invited to their home for a meal and to play canasta, and my Danish father-in-law was a good friend of his, so there was enough of a relationship whereby we could have worked out something together. Someone has suggested that I could have gone to the library and read up on the subject, but as my knowledge of Spanish was almost nil and there was not much likelihood of there being any English or American books in the library, even if there had been a library in the nearest town which was two hours drive away, that was a remote possibility. To liaise with my friend was, but it never occurred to me to ask him, and as I replied with an emphatic 'No', he obviously thought I was not interested. The other problem was that even though things were not as perfect as they should have been at home, it would have meant leaving Jackie and Carolyn for the bush. It's possible, of course, that Bill may have discussed the possibility with Jackie who may have encouraged him to persuade me to take the job as it would have been much better paid than the job in the grocery store, and would have undoubtedly led to greater things if the job had been a success. I was never a mechanic, but I had had quite a lot of experience with transport in the army and there would have been a mechanic on the site in any case. It wasn't the last time that I failed to see an opportunity staring me in the face; they've cropped up with incessant regularity throughout my life. What I didn't know at the time was that there were tribes of Montilones on the border of Venezuela and Columbia who'd killed several geologists and just badly wounded two National Guardsmen. Perhaps it was just as well I didn't go. They brought in an American engineer instead.

Some time after this happened, Jackie and I had a furious row about the conduct of her mother during her stays with us, which precipitated the parting of our ways. Everybody seemed to be delighted, especially my dear mother-in-law, to arrange for my departure. Even my boss, a Mr Ryan, who was always requesting that I sing 'When Irish Eyes are Smiling' appeared anxious to get rid of me and urged me to have a go on Ed Sullivan's show in New York. There was a general feeling that I would be much better off pursuing my career on the stage, and being of a romantic nature I was easily persuaded to have another go, after all I was only 32. When other people were half way through their working life I was still trying to prove that I was another Caruso in the making, despite having been wisely advised by professionals that I should 'go and grow tomatoes.' Mr Ryan helped me to get a visa in the American Consul's office in Puerto de la Cruz when the time came, whilst my mother-in-law arranged for me to travel as the only passenger on a Norwegian cargo ship bound for Savannah, Georgia, for a mere pittance, despite having my own cabin and taking my meals with the captain. The idea was that I should go to the U.S.A., take the 'big apple' by storm, become a star overnight on the Ed Sullivan show and when I'd arranged accommodation for the family, Jackie and Carolyn were to join me!

On the way to Savannah our ship called in at Santiago for a load of sugar. While we were waiting to be loaded up and the crew had nothing to do, the first mate decided to lead an expedition to an uninhabited island some distance from the ship and invited me to join them in hunting iguanas the size of small alligators. It was a ridiculous idea, and we spent several hours getting there in one of the lifeboats with an outboard motor. When we did, the island was infested with mosquitoes and we were devoured alive. There were some iguanas on the island, but we never got near them and when we got back to our boat the tide had gone out leaving it grounded with two sharks patrolling up and down at a distance of 30 metres from it. We had to wait for the tide to return and the sharks to become bored and head off somewhere else. It was almost dark before we left the island and when we got back to the ship the captain was livid with the first mate for risking our lives and screamed at him for the rest of the evening. I've never been so embarrassed in all my life and sought the refuge of my cabin which was at the other end of the ship. The following day we spent a few hours in Santiago going round the bars, and later that evening set off for Savannah where we arrived on a Sunday morning in time to go to church, to thank the Lord for a safe journey. Believe it or not that is exactly what I did. It was a beautiful spring morning, the church bells were ringing and it was the obvious thing to go to a Baptist church where I was more or less home from home. I shall never forget that morning.

The next day I got on a Greyhound bus and headed for New York. The journey took 27 hours and I sat next to an old lady who repeatedly told me about the day she visited the White House and dined with Harry S. Truman and his wife. 'Just ordinary folks' she said, 'used to be a shop-keeper. Showed me all over the place, he did, couldna bin a nicer guy.' Thank goodness she got off in Washington D.C.

Foolishly, I splashed out and rented an apartment in Greenwich Village. I then got in touch with an old wartime friend of Lil's who introduced me to a theatrical agent who in turn eventually got me on a show out in the sticks at the Colony Club, which I think was Jewish. I was introduced as an Australian, because the British were unpopular at the time for not allowing the Jews to return to their homeland in Palestine. I was only given short notice of my Australian origins, and this gave me a problem as all I knew of the country was that it was somewhere out near the Indian and Pacific Oceans and had a population of about ten million. When someone came round to the dressing room at the end of the show and introduced himself as one who had earned his living 'on the boards' and had done a tour of Australia, and asked 'did I know Sydney, Melbourne, Canberra and Perth?' I had to say 'No, I'm sorry, but I come from the bush and am not familiar with the big cities.' Then he told me the names of the theatres and the towns in which he had performed. It was an embarrassing couple of minutes. This followed another uncomfortable moment, for I had been taken by surprise by the compere who, when I had finished my performance, came bounding on to the stage to do an interview, again with no prior warning. He asked me what I thought of New York and I said something about not being terribly impressed but, of course, I wasn't very familiar with it, and a female voice bellowed from the auditorium 'Why don't you go home?'

I eventually had the opportunity to audition for the Ed Sullivan show. The lady who took my name and address asked me what I was going to do with the prize money, and to try and impress her I said I'd give it to the badly disabled, not realising that I was the most disabled of all! There was no prize money however. No sooner had I opened my mouth than the gentleman in charge of the auditions shouted, 'You should be in opera' and called for the next in line. He just wanted to get rid of me as I knew darned well I wasn't any good for opera because I hadn't got the range even if I had a big voice. It was his way of saying you're not good enough for our television show. I was wearing my toupee as well! It obviously didn't impress!

Soon after this I received a letter from Jackie, a letter that took me by surprise and left me devastated. She wanted a divorce. Even though we'd had troubled times because of her mother's drinking problems, we'd never even thought of a divorce. Believing I could change her mind I got on the next plane to Caracas and thence Punta de Mata, to find that, no doubt with her mother's guidance, she had begun divorce proceedings in Maturin. My first reaction was one of anger. After travelling 6,000 miles to get married, the first thing she did as soon as I was out of the way was to start divorce proceedings. It was the first time I broke down and cried. I thought how low can people get. But it wasn't all, for Jackie said 'Why don't you go home? When you were in New York you could have got on a boat.'

It hadn't entered my mind, all I wanted to do was to save my marriage, only now could I see it was a mess. If only I had ignored Jackie's mother in the first place. I hadn't the education or the preparation to provide for Jackie and Carolyn the life to which Jackie's mother was accustomed, and that was about the long and the short of it. Some men are so easily led.

My dear mother-in-law was ever ready to help, however, for she had got wind of a development which the Venezuelan Government had initiated in the bush in the west of the country, right on the other side from where the oil company was situated. To generate interest in modern farming methods, the government, with the help of some American agronomists had deforested thousands of hectares of jungle. Here they had built simple breeze-block bungalows each of three bedrooms, kitchen and comedor/sitting room, with corrugated roofs and no ceilings, and the interior walls high enough not to be looked over. Each had an outside squat toilet, or rather a hole in the ground with a concrete floor, breeze-block walls and corrugated roof. With each shack there would be 20 to 30 hectare 'parcelas' and for the immigrants being brought from the displaced camps in Germany, there would be a full complement of agricultural machinery including an International (Farmal) Tractor, 3-disc plough, set of harrowing discs and a drill for planting, all on credit. A network of roads had been built for the first stage of the development, but had not been asphalted and have remained, apart from the main road going through the Colony of Turen, as it was called in 1952, in the same state ever since.

When I returned from North America I found Lil had arranged for her newly married son and daughter-in-law to come and stay with Jackie, and as her son was also in search of something to do, together we went off to explore the possibility of putting a claim in for a piece of land in the state of Portuguese. First we had to visit the area in question, and this was no easy task as the distance from Caracas to the Colony of Turen was 400 kms and we had no transport and little cash. This left us the one option of the prehistoric long distance, uncomfortable, clapped out char-a-bancs which travelled overnight and took 12 hours to do the 400 kilometres. (40 years later these same buses are being used, but for only local services around towns.) A friend of Lil's had given us the name of a Mr Jack Clark, the foreman/supervisor of his contracting company building roads and canals in the Colony. We called on him in the first place and were able to scrounge a meal and a night's kip in the camp after reconnoitering the Colony.

We visited a Dr Sam Strebbin, an American and one of the founders, from whom we were able to gain some information. However, the first thing he asked us limeys was 'Why don't you go to one of your Colonies?' which left us speechless because circumstances had landed us there. I suppose we could have gone to British Guiana which was only next door to Venezuela, but we were in Venezuela and hadn't intended leaving. Dr Strebbin could only suggest the correct procedure for acquiring a 'parcela' or farm and told us to go to the Institute of Agrario Nacional in Caracas—the National Agrarian Institute—where we could make an application. Our journey was not completely pointless, but we did not learn much by making such a long trip. We hadn't got any transport and without it one could not gain much more information. There were two other Americans in the Colony who had already been given 'parcelas', brothers by the name of Boring, but they were kilometres away, so that it was impossible to visit them. They could have given us some valuable information as they had been through the grind of applying, but were obviously in the money before settling in, as one was a pilot and was employed fumigating the crops.

There was talk of Jackie and I making it up again if I could get a 'parcela', but now I realise that was just pie in the sky and a carrot to get me to the other side of the country and out of the way. At the time it seemed a genuine possibility but plans had already been made. It wasn't long before she was married again to an American engineer, whom she'd known even before I had gone to Venezuela.

I remained in Caracas, staying in a small pension where I met a Norwegian, Robert Nygaard, and his wife, whose name escapes me, who were also applying for a 'parcela'. They'd already approached the Institute, made their application and were now making regular journeys to the office. The following day we all went together and as I could speak English and a bit of Spanish, and they neither, I became the group spokesman. Fortunately I made contact with a Doctor Agronomo who could speak English and was a Colombian. Nothing had yet been decided about the Nygaard's application and all I had to do was to provide a reference of my farming experience. This took me several days to organise, because not being a quick thinker it did not dawn on me that I could write my own reference. But once I had, I wrote it in the third person as if by a family friend. It mentioned that I'd been brought up on a farm, though not mentioning that we did all our work with horses, and that I had been a farming student on my uncle's dairy farm for two years. Also that I had had considerable experience driving machinery. The reference being typed I returned to the Oficina del Instituto Agrario and presented my reference to Doctor Agronomo who suggested that I return in a week's time.

The following week all three of us returned and waited several hours before anyone was free to come and see us. Eventually our friend Dr Lopez, a Colombian who could speak English, had a moment to spare and came out to see us and explained that there was no machinery available for us and no money to purchase it at that stage, but that if we could provide our own, our applications would be considered.

We returned to the pension and talked it over that evening. They could not speak English very well and I, of course, could not speak Norwegian at all, but we managed to work something out which with me being so dense, as per usual, was to my detriment in the end. At the time I was almost broke having spent the $2,000 I was required to possess before being admitted to the US as an immigrant, so that to put our scheme into operation I had to return to Punta de Mata to see some old friends. The idea was that we should buy a tractor between us on which we would have to pay the deposit of Bs 5,000, the equivalent of £500. As Robert had no close friends from whom to seek help, the contract would have to be in his name so that he could go to the Norwegian Ambassador explaining that he alone was buying the tractor and wanted to borrow 5,000 bolivars.

I borrowed the £250 for my half share from an old friend and then proceeded to Agropsa, the Fordson distributors in Caracas, and presented our proposition. This was eagerly accepted as agricultural machinery distributors were falling over themselves to supply machinery to prospective 'parceleros' of the Colony of Turen. They were not so keen later on!

Being thus in possession of something more concrete we returned to the Institute just as the office was closing for lunch one day, but managed to corner Dr Lopez and explain that we were able to provide a tractor between us if they'd give us each a parcela. 'Muy bien, venga la semana proxima',—'Very well, come next week.'

The following week we returned once again, but after waiting for two hours we were told that nothing had been decided and 'venga la semana proxima.'

Once again we went back to the Institute Agrario Nacional the following week and were advised that the Director was now on holiday, and that he wouldn't be back until the end of September. It was then the 7th so it meant waiting three weeks. It was all right for Robert and his wife as they were working, he on construction and she as a nurse, but I was already finding it difficult to survive and manage on one meal a day in the pension.

At the beginning of October we tried again, when Dr Lopez explained that there was only one parcela available and that they had decided to give it to me, which caused a tremendous hullabaloo. Robert's wife went berserk and began a long tirade in Norwegian which only her husband understood. Although I didn't understand I perceived the significance of what she was saying, they had applied before I had and were first in the queue, and as such were quite rightly entitled to the available parcela. To calm Robert's wife's fears I told them that there was no problem, 'No hay problema, you can have the parcela, you were here first, if the Institute will agree.' It transpired that the reason why they gave me the parcela was that I had done all the talking, but my explanation settled the problem and they signed for the parcela. The Nygaard's told me that until I had been granted my parcela, I could share everything with them and vice-versa. I would share in the work and in return they would give me an allowance from the credit received from the Institute. Each crop was financed at stages by the Institute which would enable us to survive on a small living allowance.

The next step was to go and see about the Fordson tractor, on which we needed to pay a deposit of Bs5,000, leaving a balance of Bs25,000 to be paid in three installments over the next 18 months, which meant after the next three harvests, though of what crop they were going to be we had no idea. The only problem was that Robert, unbeknown to me, had had no success with his ambassador. From what developed later I doubt whether he had ever been to see him. Agropsa, the distributor, was nevertheless keen to complete a sale and the following day I drove the tractor out of the firm's yard and began a journey that was to last for 36 hours, from that morning through the following night and all next day, with Robert sitting on the mudguard. His wife had gone on by bus.

In Caracas I had bought a straw hat to protect my bald head from the sun and on our first stop in Los Teques in the hills for a pepsi-cola, I left my lovely new straw hat on the seat. When we came out of the cafe it had gone. I had forgotten where I was. Although at that time in Venezuela you could almost leave your wallet on the doorstep, straw hats were an exception.

Before going to the parcela itself Robert wanted to call on a Danish friend who as well as being a parcelero was the Colony's carpenter. About 200 yards before we arrived at the Dane's home Robert said he wanted to drive. He'd been watching me for the last 36 hours and decided that he could now drive the tractor. We proceeded at a snail's pace for the last 200 yards!

The Dane had made a bed, a table and four chairs for Robert and his wife and would deliver them to their parcela. Robert picked up his wife who had arrived at the Dane's that morning and with each sitting on the mudguards, I drove down to the parcela, which was 30 kilometres away at Camino 6, Road 6.

13
La Colonia de Turen

Everything went swimmingly for two weeks although I was sleeping on the floor until we got our, or Robert's, first credit, and then I was able to purchase a hammock. Then, perhaps the resentment that had been building up ever since I'd met them came to the fore and Robert's wife decided that she wasn't going to cook for me any more. This meant I had to go to Turen on the Fordson and buy a kerosene cooker and some groceries and cook for myself in my room. That proved to be just the start. Some time later it was decided that the credit wasn't enough for all three and as a result I was no longer required to help on the farm. Whilst I looked for work on someone else's parcela, I kept myself alive with a piece of string and a safety pin fishing in a stream running through the jungle a few kilometres away. There were always odd jobs that one could pick up on the surrounding farms and one was pulling beans which were left in a heap to dry so that they could be put through the threshing machine, or binder, drawn by a tractor. Then there was my old Canadian friend, Mitchell, who was well in his fifties, who was always good for a touch if you'd given him a hand with something, which was often the case as he was a bit over weight and didn't like to stay out in the sun for too long at a time!

Meanwhile, I made frequent trips to Caracas on the old bus to pester the life out of Dr Lopez and soon after Christmas 1952 he gave me the good news that there was a parcela available for me. I returned the same night feeling on top of the world and the following morning went straight to see Dr Branco, 'El Jefe encargado de las tierras' — Head of land management, who drove me to see two parcelas from which I could choose the one I wanted. Unfortunately, I picked the wrong one, the one that was largely deforested and cleared, whilst the other had the much better soil but only 15 hectares had been deforested. We just viewed them from the road as Dr Branco did not suggest that we get out of the jeep to go and have a close look.

The parcela was No. 364 of Carretera M — Road M — which backed onto the jungle and howling monkeys. The Cano Guamal (Guamal Canal) streamed along the end of the parcela and it was bordered by a 20 metre wind break — 'un rompe viento' — of jungle. It comprised 38 hectares and contained three types of soil, most of which was heavy and the rest light and medium, with drainage canals of 2 m x 1.5 m to the front and each side. The house had not yet been built. That, however, was no problem as there was one partially built on the opposite side of the road, with no windows or doors and, as yet, no concrete floor. It had the usual outside toilet. In those days under President Perez Jimenez, it was quite safe to sleep in a house with no doors, but not today. So, without permission, after collecting my bits and pieces from the Nygaards, I dossed down, sorry up, because of the hammock, in one of the rooms in the unfinished bungalow which was to be my home until my own bungalow was built.

Until such time as the credit arrived, I amused myself by tidying up what I could of the parcela as there was a great deal of rubbish lying about that could be collected and burnt. I also set fire to the trees and brush that had been felled and pushed up into four rows and which had to be cleared off the land so that its full potential could be enjoyed. It took a couple of years before it was all cleared away.

'El Banco Agrario' — The Agrarian Bank — advanced the credit for planting maize which for the 38 hectares on my farm amounted to Bs10,000, £1,000. This was to be dished out in four stages; preparing the ground, planting, cultivating and harvesting. The Institute provided extra credit for dusting and spraying the 'gusanos'—caterpillars or grubs—on the maize which was required at least twice and possibly three times.

My only problem was getting my hands on the tractor in which I had invested £250, but Robert was also very busy at the same time, so it meant waiting until he could spare it. Suddenly, to my utter amazement, 'our' tractor appeared on the forecourt of my next door neighbour's house. Jorge Petrick whose brother was a neighbour of Robert's, had borrowed it. He'd also been given a parcela without machinery and probably had promised that he was going to buy his own. But 'our' Fordson Tractor by now had begun to have hiccups due to its journey at top speed over 400 kilometres from Caracas. It hadn't dawned on me at the time that an engine shouldn't be driven at such a speed over such a distance in so short a time.

On approaching my next door neighbour's farm I discovered that 'our' dearly beloved Fordson tractor was in pieces. Jorge, a Russian, considered himself somewhat of a mechanic and had promised Robert to repair it if he could use it and had taken it away. Just to make sure that I wasn't going to drive it away whilst he and his wife were out, he started to take it to pieces. However, I sought the assistance of Jorge's neighbour, Andres Zeiberg, a Latvian, who knew a bit more about the mechanism of a tractor than your's truly. We reassembled it and I drove it away to my farm whilst Jorge and his wife were still not at home. Of course the tractor was useless. It could hardly pull itself let alone a set of discs, so my only solution was to take it to Janis and Leopoldo to get it repaired. (Both were Croats from what was then Yugoslavia and are now dead. Leopoldo was murdered for a few bolivares). No sooner had I got the tractor repaired than Robert and his wife were on the doorstep pestering me for it, before I had had much time to use it. I had by now obtained some implements from the Institute. This, of course, was an impossible situation. I can deal with my own sex, but when Robert's wife began screaming abuse in a language I did not understand and in a raucous, strident voice with which there were few to compare, I gave up and told them to take the bloody tractor away.

I've met and known some women in my time, but she 'took the biscuit'. How a man can become involved with such a bitch amazes me, but we all make mistakes; she must have had some hold on him other than a wedding ring; there must have been a dark side to his life because under normal circumstances no man's life is worth the torment she gave him. Within two years Robert and his wife were thrown off the 'parcela' and out of the Colony of Turen because of her drunken scenes in the main office of the Agrarian Institute when they were trying to collect some credits. It wasn't always easy to get some money when you needed it as for some reason it had not been allocated by the government and one had to be patient. Sometimes one would spend days at a time in a queue waiting to collect to no avail and have to return the following day, and the next day and next. If you hadn't any money to buy groceries it was tough luck, especially if like many you had a family to look after. You needed patience, and Robert's wife had none. They had a lovely 'parcela' with excellent soil especially suitable for maize, producing 3,000 to 4,000 kilos a hectare at 60 'centavos' a kilo on 50 hectares, or sesame—'ajonjoli'—of 1,000 kilos per hectare at 1 bolivar per kilo. Other 'parceleros' farming in the same road 'made a bomb'. I met one, an American and his wife, when I was in Venezuela recently, who lived in the same road not far from Robert's who'd wangled a second 'parcela' making a total 100 hectares of excellent land. At one time he'd gone in for cattle farming, but the local villagers suffered from hunger, especially of meat, and he noticed an occasional reduction in numbers of his herd of brahmins, so he decided to sell the remainder while he'd still got them! Overall, however, they did very well and were on the point of selling up and retiring to Barbados. Robert should have got rid of his wife and soldiered on by himself with the help of a squaw and he could have retired as well. Instead, one day when I was in the town of Turen doing some shopping who should be sitting in the passenger seat of a lorry, but Robert with 'our' tractor in the back. He looked straight ahead treating me with utter disdain and contempt although he could not have helped seeing me. He didn't even wave and say good-bye

Bernard, thank you for 'our' tractor! I never saw it again and I believe that they went somewhere over the other side of the country to the State of Bolivar near what is today Guyana.

The day after I told Robert to take the tractor, I jumped on shank's pony, hitched a lift to Turen roughly 20 kilometres from the 'parcela', caught a bus to Barquisimeto 90 kilometres away which was the nearest agency for farm machinery, and bought a John Deere 'G'. This was one of the best two cylinder tractors in the world with an absolutely fantastic engine to listen to. I bought it without paying a deposit, explaining that I'd just got a 'parcela' in La Colonia de Turen. 'No hay problema Senor,' said the salesman, 'Uds. puede pagar con la cosecha'—'There's no problem Sir, you can pay with the harvest.' The tractor was even delivered by the agency.

Now I could go to work without hindrance and without a drooling lunatic of a woman breathing down my neck. I prepared the available ground and planted maize with the International drill I had scrounged from the Institute, on credit. The seeds were also obtained from the Institute, on credit, and the bank had already dished out credit for the first two stages of the crop. I was laughing, and getting into debt! Ruffo, an Ecuadorian friend who incidentally knew my dear mother-in-law, proffered a 2,000 litre gasoline tank rent free as long as he could supply the petrol. 'No hay problema.' I probably paid for that tank a number of times but when you are skint they've got you by the short hairs.

The Italian contractors had by this time built my bungalow; the electricity had been laid on, whilst water was delivered weekly into two 200 litre drums outside on the road. Although the drums had lids on them, because of the gravel roads the water always had a nice little film of dust on the top.

I slung my hammock in one of the rooms, put the two ring kerosene cooker on the concrete worktop in the kitchen and had bought the basic necessities of life such as black beans and rice— my protein and carbohydrates. The Venezuelans of whatever social status live forever on beans and rice. If you live in the country and haven't a fridge you can't be forever running off to the butcher's to buy meat, so beans are a good substitute and a lot healthier. There was also an abundance of fresh fruit in Venezuela including oranges, grapefruit, lemons, bananas, and plantains or 'platanos', the latter being used more like a vegetable which the Venezuelans fry or boil as well as eat raw like a banana. 'Lechosa' or pawpaw was a delicious fruit and also the mango. Melons of all varieties were produced in abundance. Then there were the more exotic fruits like tamarind, guava, 'guanabano' or custard apple, pineapples, 'nispero', 'parchita', 'parcha' and 'torona', the last four of which I have no translation.

Fresh meat could be obtained, if there was nothing else to do, by stalking deer on the plain down by the Portuguese river, though it was a longish ride by tractor along miles of jungle tracks. Two Polish brothers and myself used to drive down during the late afternoon in time to stalk the deer with a spotlight connected to the tractor battery. On reflection, after nearly 40 years, the experience fills me with remorse and would be extremely offensive to me now, but one of us drove the tractor while Casimiro held the spotlight looking for the deer. The other aimed to shoot the deer between the eyes when they shone like headlamps as the spotlight picked them out. We seldom killed the animal outright. Many a deer must have crawled away only to die a painful death as it was very difficult to find them in the long elephant grass. We never brought home more than one on each occasion because we hadn't the facilities to store the meat.

Another favourite pursuit was hunting wild boar in the jungle which we did during the day. These could sometimes prove very dangerous, as wild pigs will tear you to pieces if they get you in a corner. On one occasion when we were out together with a couple of Germans (I was the only Englishman in the Colony of 27 nationalities) when we heard one of them shouting for help. As we approached the direction from where the cries of anxiety emanated, which proved to be an 800 year old Saman—Rain tree—we could see about ten or twelve wild boar at its foot up which Hans was sitting on a branch. We had only one twelve-bore between us and Hans didn't have it as he was one of the 'beaters'. I was the other, so Casimiro did the only thing possible and fired at the little pigs, dropping one and wounding two or three of the others, scattering them in all directions. When they saw Jorge, who wasn't very big, they decided to go after him. Luckily for him there was another old Saman near at hand which he had no problem in climbing and which probably saved him from at least being cut about the ankles. The Germans, forever thinking primarily of number one, gutted the pig and took it home for their family. It was their gun anyway.

It proved difficult to grow maize because of the heavy typical, tropical, torrential rain which sometimes poured incessantly for days on end. It destroyed most of the maize, but there were patches in more elevated positions that had survived which needed cleaning in between the rows. It was not possible to get the tractor onto the ground as it was saturated, so instead I employed a couple of peons with machetes. One, Molgado, decided it would be more convenient for him, rather than walking home over the Guamal Canal at the foot of the 'parcela' and on to his rancho in the village in the jungle, to sling his hammock in my bungalow. This proved to be quite a good idea as he was a good cook, always adding some strange condiments to the beans which added relish to the food. Occasionally he returned excitedly to the house with a creature of the forest which he had hunted such as a 'cachicama'—an armadillo, or a 'puerco espino'—a porcupine, that he would then barbecue on an outside wood fire. 'Chiguires'—capibarras, the largest member of the rodent family, sometimes roamed along the canal leaving its footprints, but that is as near as we could get to it. I should add that although the capibarra is a member of the rodent family it is quite edible.

At about this time, with the idea of providing regular meat and eggs to supplement our rations, I bought some white leghorn chicks, although my parcel of land was more suitable to ducks, and we built a chicken house for them with palm trunks and a corrugated iron roof. This didn't prevent them from breaking out and walking about in knee-deep mud and water, and probably because of this they contracted some sort of disease and began to drop like nine-pins. We caught one or two in time and put them in the pot, but most of the fifty went the same way. It didn't require much thought to decide that my farm was not suitable for chickens. I didn't go in for ducks, but Molgado acquired a number of 'morrocoys'—boxturtles, which he put in a stone enclosure which he built for them. He used to feed them on corn and greenery he'd collect from the parcela. 'Morrocoys' are a regular delicacy for people living in the forest, but disaster overtook us once again and the boxturtles disappeared one night when we were out. Someone else had been keeping their eye on them. The same thing happened to a deer that I'd paid £1 for when it was a few days old. I'd made a corral for her, named her Bambi and didn't intend her to be eaten, but when she was fully grown someone stole her. We actually discovered who the culprit was and reported him to the police. He was eventually summoned to appear in court and I, as the owner of the deer, was asked by the judge how much the deer was worth and I told him the equivalent of £50. The judge ordered the thief to pay me 50 bolivares a month until the debt was cleared, but no doubt the judge got the money because I didn't receive a bolivar!

The maize harvest that season proved to be a disaster leaving me up to my eyes in debt, but for the moment no one was threatening any drastic measures.

The next season was the dry one, from November to April, and we prepared to plant sesame, another crop unsuitable for the soil on my land, but the Institute's agronomists disregarded this minor detail and recommended the usual credits, again generously handed out at the appropriate stage. The problem with sesame is that you have to plant it when the soil is moist enough to germinate the seeds. If it is too dry the seeds will not sprout so that you have to disc again and replant. Heavy soil take a lot of working down before you get the right seed bed for such small seeds and while you are going over and over the ground trying to work it down, the tropical sun is beating down and drying it up. In common parlance you are knackered unless you have the good fortune to have a miraculous downfall of rain. It does sometimes happen, but not for me. I planted three times during that first sesame season and finally obtained a germination on the lighter soil. It never rains during the dry season so that the crop had to depend entirely on moisture in the ground. It helps to cultivate as you loosen the soil, so preventing it from cracking as it is wont to do and drying out even more. The outcome of this was a little more encouraging than the maize and we harvested 10,000 kilos off about 28 hectares—ten of the hectares were still taken up with the deforested trees and bush which had not yet been burned off. Parcelas of soil more suitable for sesame of the same hectarage would have produced as much as 800 to 1,000 kilos to the hectare. One or two Germans I knew in another area of the Colony sold their parcels of land after five years because they were lucky enough to have acquired the right ones; the right soil for producing two crops a year, maize during the wet season and sesame during the dry. One of the Germans sold the key to the parcela for the equivalent of £2,000 together with the machinery and transferred the parcels of land to the name of the purchaser, quite legally. He returned to Germany and bought an apartment building and a shoe factory. What luck!

For the following planting I planted half maize and half rice. This was the first time I'd had experience of the latter, which is planted the same as wheat, oats or barley in this country except that we planted the drills 35 centimetres apart to enable the peons to clean in between the rows as it would be impossible to get onto the land with a tractor and cultivator during the wet season. At that time there was no such thing as a weed-killer in the Colony, though experiments were made later with 24D which killed only the wide-leafed variety of weeds. They now have a comprehensive variety of weed-killers, but in 1954 or thereabouts the machete was the weed-killer. To hire 'obreros'—workers, you drove your tractor and trailer down to the Saman tree in Turen where workers wanting work would assemble and wait to be hired. This Saman was a monster of a tree and must have been a thousand years old; it was a beautiful tree and much to my horror and disgust I've noticed during my recent visit to the Colony that the Council vandals had ordered that it should be cut down; the town isn't the same place without it. To be in time to pick up any 'obreros', I'd have to start from home at 3 a.m. to get there by 4.30 a.m., otherwise there wouldn't be anyone left, and you'd have had a wasted journey. The men would want to start work at 6 a.m. so that they could finish at noon before it became too hot. The peons were dab hands with their machetes and would slash the weeds in-between the rows, but I also thought they were cutting the heads off the rice. Not being familiar with rice, I didn't realise that the rice had not yet produced the tassel so that the men were not actually cutting off the heads of the rice only the top of the plant. But I'm afraid I lost my temper with one or two before I realised my mistake, which could have endangered my well-being because some of the workers could be rather quick-tempered and wouldn't think twice before taking a swipe at you with the machete, the all-purpose tool, as I was to learn from a later experience.

When the men finished at noon they had to be returned to the Saman. Some men with lorries started up as contractors and gathered together a bunch of men to carry out the work of cleaning rice but, of course, it would cost somewhat more than if you organised it yourself. The men were paid about Bs2 a 'hilera'—a row—the equivalent of 4/- and they would clean ten rows of 800 metres each, if they were lucky, at a trot. The peons would be paid the same whether they were working for a contractor or directly for the 'parcelero'.

I managed to save a bit of money from the credits received from the Institute and bought myself an old Land-Rover—being an Englishman I had to buy something made in England. Using it to go on my first ever visit to a soirée in the Social Club in the centre of the Colony, I was stopped half way by Jorge who stood crying on the side of the road and asked me to fetch the National Guard as someone had killed his sister-in-law and her three sons. I could hardly believe my ears, but I went to the National Guard post in the centre of the Colony and told them what had happened, and returned with them to Jorge's parcela. His mother and brother, Casimiro, whose wife and sons had been killed, were away for the day. When we entered the house we were faced with the worst scene I have ever seen in my life, including six years of war. Jorge's sister-in-law and her sons were lying in a pool of blood in the corner of the living room, and it appeared that they had been slashed to death with a machete whilst they were alone in the house sometime during the day. It was now 7 o'clock at night so that a lot of time had been wasted, and to make matters worse the Guards had not brought an ambulance, so that I had to go to the hospital to fetch one with a doctor and two nurses. One of the sons was miraculously still breathing, though unconscious, and they were all put into the ambulance and taken to the hospital. It later transpired that the brothers had had a dispute with a tractor driver over payment for his services, but the man was caught and sentenced to life imprisonment. However, two years later the brothers' mother saw him walking about in a nearby town as a free man. (Another friend of mine had a similar dispute with an 'obrero' over his wages and he was attacked with the machete almost severing his left leg and spent twelve months in hospital.)

It was late before I got into my hammock that night. I awoke the following morning to the sounds of machetes cutting the grass on the side of the road, but when I put my head through the window there was no one there.

There was unsurprisingly a lot of resentment towards us foreigners for the simple reason that when the jungle was cleared by the government to establish the colony of 600 parcelas with an average of 35 hectares of land each, a great number of 'campesinos' or 'conuceros', named after the patch of ground that they had cleared in the jungle, were ejected from their 'ranchito', their little house made of mud and wattle with a roof of palm leaves. (In the United States a conuco was a patch of ground given to slaves; a maize field.) Much the same is happening in the Amazon today. It appears that , about two years after the founding of the Colony, someone took it upon himself to organise an invasion of the Colony by the people who had lost their patches of ground and attack the police post as they saw the police as their persecutors. Three of the Guards were killed, along with five peasants. Even after 40 years the 'campesino'—countryman or woman—calls a foreigner 'musiu' which is a derivation of the French word 'monsieur' but which is used in a derogatory manner.

This time I had a fairly good harvest although the expenses were high as the weeds grew fast and furious, especially on the higher ground and though we suffered several attacks of the 'gusanos' which required the use of an airplane to do the spraying as it was impossible to spray by tractor because of the sodden ground. We probably harvested 50,000 kilos from the available land and it was delivered to the silos in the Colony belonging to the Institute against the credits received and allowing further credit to be drawn. Provided you showed willing you were never short of a bob or two if you needed it. One old friend of mine, a Canadian aged about 55, always had a problem in obtaining credit because he never planted his crops in time. So he fetched an armchair and sat outside the office, reading a book. His wife, who was Venezuelan, used to bring him his meals and he slept in the chair with a blanket round him. After three days the Institute gave in, and advanced him Bs500, enough to buy some groceries for a couple of weeks.

However, it was not always easy to obtain credit with the Institute as it depended upon the government coughing up the allocated finance to the Institute at the time required. It, therefore, sometimes made it necessary to seek credit elsewhere and though I personally did not become so involved, one person who leaped in to fill the void was a Jew from Czechoslovakia who owned two cinemas in the area. He was prepared to advance credit to anyone provided they in turn sold him their crop at a price he dictated which, of course, was below the market price. He would also charge 20% interest on the money he loaned and would make sure the 'parcelero' had the possibility of a harvest, employing a 'perito'— an appraiser—to visit the 'parcela' or 'parcelas' before the loan was agreed. The great attraction to the farmer of this arrangement was the relative speed with which finance was advanced. Meanwhile the Czech disposed of his cinemas and gained the confidence of hundreds of 'parceleros', developing a substantial business and employing lawyers to take care of the legal side of the transactions. There was always a delay in payment once the harvest had been delivered, but eventually the farmers got their money. This went on satisfactorily for several years, the business building up all the while. Then, after one harvest the Czechoslovakian disappeared with millions of bolivares belonging to the 'parceleros'. No one knew where he had gone; 30 years later they still don't know what happened to him and their money. The lawyers were jailed for up to five years.

There were other means of obtaining credit, such as planting yellow corn for a feed and fowl company, Protenal. They gave, or rather sold you the seeds, on credit of course, and if you required some money, they would advance you a few thousand bolivares provided you'd got a good stand. A local merchant once sold me some black peas to plant, but they did not even sprout, so they must have passed their sell by date. As they were a dry season crop, it wasn't possible to plant something else instead. It was too late. The merchant obviously knew they were no good because he never chased me for payment.

I was now in the dry season of 1955/1956 and getting the 'parcela' completely cleared of deforested timber and bush, having burnt all of it over the course of time and had been able to borrow a leveller from the Institute to spread the soil evenly over the land, smoothing over the mounds of soil and holes where the trees had been. The parcel of land now looked a picture, cleared of all the rubbish and as well as levelling it we—a Greek was helping me as a tractor driver, and I still owe him Bs 500 by the way—borrowed a 'bigroma', a set of 30" heavy discs, and prepared the ground well for planting rice during the wet season. We were all ready and just waiting for a good downfall of rain so the rice would get a good start, and the only other thing missing was the drill which my next door neighbour, Jose D'alisandre, an Italian, had borrowed to plant his rice. Ever obliging I had said 'Como no, Jose, Llevala sembradora. Estoy a sus ordenes.' — 'Of course, Jose, take it. I am at your service!' But, when I went to look for it, it was standing by the house doing nothing. Of course, he too was waiting for the rain. So I had what turned out to be a good idea. I'd plant in the dry soil and hope it would soon rain; it was due any time anyway. Jose was very annoyed when I said I would have to take the planter away and I don't think we exchanged two words from that day to this since. (There are two ways to lose friends — by lending them money and machinery.) But take the drill away I did and planted in dry soil. Three days later it poured with rain for 48 hours and a week after it had rained I got a tremendous germination. Like the shepherd said about his sheep; to look at those lovely rows of rice plants when the dew was on them first thing in the morning and with the sun shining on them from the west, was my delight. I can see them even now 41 years later and wish I could live those days over again.

At about this time I bumped into a countryman of mine — at least he said he was — who had a big farm outside the Colony which was nothing to do with the government. He suggested that he would give me some land on which I could plant anything I wanted in return for the hire of my tractor and myself as manager. It sounded a good deal to me, especially as I could choose any piece of land I preferred. I chose about 40 hectares of good soil on which I planted more rice.

Meanwhile the Greek left to start up a 'rag' business and went to another part the country selling clothes from a suitcase; he eventually married a Venezuelan, sired a football team and ran a supermarket. Camillo Nasuti, an Italian, came to work for me as a tractor driver as I now had to run Griff Christian's farm as well as my own, and he had four tractors of various makes with Venezuelan tractor drivers and a mechanic. Most of Griff's 400 hectares had been planted with yellow corn for Protenal; they manufactured the feed from the maize and hatched chickens for sale all over the country. All that remained was for me to supervise the cultivating and dusting against the 'gusanos'. The land was such that you could get the tractors on it to cultivate the day after it rained. I don't think there was a hectare of clay soil on the whole farm; it was exceptionally good soil.

The 400 arable hectares were only part of his farm, he had another 3,600 hectares of jungle containing valuable timber which was felled and hauled off to the timber yards for the home market and export, all of which was supervised by the 'Jefe grande'—Griff. He accommodated himself in a hammock in my house when visiting his farm and partook of the bacon and eggs I provided for the big chief's breakfast; he loved cornflakes too!

One day, to my utter surprise, I received a letter from my ex-mother-in-law inviting me to visit them in their apartment in Caracas as my daughter was in town and she thought I might like to see her for the first time in three years. My old jalopy was too rickety to drive to Caracas, so it was to be the old faithful prehistoric charabanc again, the 12 hour journey arriving at 9 a.m. in Silencio Square in the centre of Caracas. After a breakfast of black coffee and an 'arepa'—deliciously hot maize bread with meat and cheese, and a wash and brush up in the restaurant, I drew a deep breath and proceeded to John and Lil's apartment in the east of the city. Carolyn had grown quite a bit and had forgotten me; she was playing with a toy as I remember and didn't even lift her head as I walked into the apartment, and Lil didn't say who I was. I suppose she was rather hoping that Carolyn wouldn't remember me so that it would be much easier to carry out their plan. Jackie and her new husband, Murfin, were also in town of course, though this had not been made known to me in the correspondence. It was all nicely planned. When I took my leave and we descended in the lift in the apartment block, who should be arriving in the foyer but Jackie and her husband both of whom completely ignored me. Indeed when John and Murfin turned round and went out for a drink to the Danish Club, Jackie called out after him 'you won't be late, will you darling?' and she and her mother got into the lift and went up to the apartment without a word. Jay was left standing there like an idiot. What bloody fools some of us are! As well as being idiots we are made to look like them. I had no idea of what was planned at the time, but when I later discovered that they had gone to the United States it became clear that they had kidnapped Carolyn and taken her out of the country without my permission.

This was to be confirmed 36 years later when I went to the States to visit Carolyn. Because her grandmother lived only a few streets away she was there too and said to Carolyn 'of course, we kidnapped you out of Venezuela.' I had refused to reply to any of Lil's letters for years. Whilst I was in Albuquerque Lil was taken to hospital and died two weeks later so I was very pleased I had seen her before she passed away. Jackie had died not long before. In the meantime she had divorced Murfin and married for the third time to a man who remained loyal to her during a long and painful illness.

Being only human I decided to go and have a drink to cheer myself up and found a bar in Sabana Grande where there were lots of girls. No, you are wrong, it wasn't a brothel, but the next best thing, what they call in Portugal a 'Boite' where you can have as much company as you like as long as you kept ordering the champagne, which I did until closing time around 3 a.m. By this time had worked up quite a relationship with a lovely blue-eyed, brainless blonde from Belgium who had given me the impression that I could spend the night with her, saying that I could call a taxi and we'd go home. When we got to her apartment at the top of Avenida Urdaneta she disappeared into the apartment block and I lost her. I'd spent about Bs800, the equivalent of £80, just to be made a fool of yet again. We never learn. Someone who was having a drink all by himself in the same bar had come over to me and said 'Uds es un idiota!' — 'You are an idiot', which rang in my ears all the way back to the Colony of Turen in the old bus.

When the rice was about 15 centimetres high we had the most marvellous flood after days of heavy rain, and I woke up to find that we were surrounded by swirling muddy waters almost coming into the shack. I had made a bridge of palm trees which I'd cut out of the 'windbreak' and it had been completely washed away, the roadside canal being full and running over. The Portuguese river had burst its banks and flooded the Guamal Canal at the end of my parcel of land, which in turn had burst its banks, bringing with it all the silt from the virgin forest and fertilising the soil. In a few weeks the rice was a magnificent sight, green and rich. Most of the weeds had been covered and killed by the water so that the rice was able to make good progress unimpaired and it was not necessary to contract workers to clean the rice. The only problem I had was with the 'gusanos' and we disposed of them in quick succession with D.D.T. which was permitted in those days and sprayed on the grubs by plane.

The rice outside the Colony on Griff's farm needed attention as the soil was light and produced a lot of weeds, so that as I had not used my credit for cleaning the rice on my 'parcela' I drew it from the Institute unbeknown to them to weed the rice on Griff's farm. On this occasion I employed a contractor to weed the rice as Camillo and I had our hands full working the two farms. It too required spraying as the grubs attack wherever they find a juicy young plant and I managed to fiddle that on the credit provided by the good old Institute!

Griff did not spend the whole time on the farm, just one week a month. The rest he spent with his family in Caracas, where they ran another business. When he wasn't in town he liked to relax in my bungalow reading a book after breakfast. He'd probably make himself many cups of tea and another breakfast at about 11 a.m. I suspect, because the bacon and eggs seemed to disappear very quickly! He used to enjoy his week of relaxation as he had a nagging, organising wife from whom he liked to escape.

During one of his visits the boss suggested that we take a box of food to some friends of his mechanic who came from Lithuania. It seems that the husband had hung himself to escape his nagging wife and the family was struggling to survive. One of the daughters who was 19 years of age had a year old son which was bad news for me; not the son, but the daughter, Irena. We were instantly attracted to each other and unknown to Griff, who I later discovered fancied her himself, I paid the family frequent visits.

Never in my wildest dreams had I envisioned when I borrowed £250 to put down on a tractor that I was one day going to harvest 200,000 kilos of rice worth Bs120,000 or £12,000. This was an undreamed of fortune in 1956, but through bad management and inexperience I overstretched myself. First I bought another tractor, a Massey-Harris 44, without paying a penny or one bolivar deposit. Then a Massey-Harris 90 Special, again without a deposit. Then my next door neighbour, whose brother-in-law was a chap by the name of Jose Benitez, a Venezuelan, persuaded me that as I had such a good harvest I should buy a new car.

'Si chico, pero yo no tengo dinero.' — 'Yes mate, but I haven't any money yet.'

'No se preocupe, no problema.' — 'Don't worry, that is no problem.' 'Puede pagar despues de la cosecha' — 'You can pay after the harvest.' And we all trooped to Caracas in Jose's car and returned to the Colony in my enormous, brand new Station Wagon of flaming red worth about £1,200 without paying a penny deposit.

'No importa, Uds, puede pagar despues de la cosecha' — 'Never mind, you can pay after the harvest.' You could always pay after the harvest.

Not content with another tractor, a combine harvester and a brand new Ford station wagon, the Secretary to the Director in the Colony said that he knew someone who had a good lorry for sale that I could buy on tick. He said I would need a lorry to transport all the rice I was going to harvest and that his friend would let me have it dirt cheap. 'Muy bien' I said. 'Very well,' 'vamos a comprar' — 'let's go and buy.' Of course, this was something that I had never come across before. I never dreamt that you could be a commission agent as well as having a regular job, but this is what these people were. They had obviously been approached by someone who had offered them a commission if they could sell something to a 'parcelero'. So, I acquired a small lorry that was no use for hauling ten tons of rice and again didn't even pay a dime deposit. My 'Institute rice' was eventually delivered to the silos by myself with tractor and trailer, and the 'private rice' by seasoned lorry drivers to private silos 50 kilometres distant.

That was not all! A big French farmer from Martinique who had a 'hacienda' — ranch or farm — adjoining my friend's, Griff, told me that he had a friend who owned 50 hectares about 30 kilometres from the Colony at a place called Piritu and was anxious to return to France, and would sell me the land cheap at Bs300 a hectare for a quick sale! It only needed deforesting, that's all! Without measuring it and by just walking over it where possible, and not knowing what sort of soil it had, I bought it, to be paid for 'after the harvest'. At this point I had no idea how much rice I was going to harvest. Everybody said that it was 'un tronco de cosecha' — a fantastic harvest — but exactly how many kilos I had no idea, although the price was already fixed at Bs0.60 a kilo. People said I'd get 3,000 kilos a hectare, but with it being the first planting that most people in my area had had, even the chief agronomist of Zone 4, our zone, hadn't much idea what the yield would be. The varieties planted locally were zenith and century patna; the former being a tall heavy headed plant would easily fall down with heavy rain and strong wind, and the latter, which I preferred and was my choice as luck would have it, because no deep thought had been given to the matter — one would hardly expect that — was short and sturdy and was not easily blown over. Even Griff, who from many disappointments was sceptical about the end product, was impressed. Apart from the flood we had the usual 150 centimetres of rain which is what you need for rice; rice under irrigation produces even more, but at that stage in the Colony no one could afford the equipment or some, the expense of drilling a bore-hole.

Irena and I were continuing our relationship and they had now moved into a spare house of a Polish family who had two parcels of land, so that I saw much more of her and being the owner of a posh new Ford station wagon we liked to go for a drive now and again. One evening when we had returned to their house, Irena's mother was filled with incandescent rage for some reason or another and, leaving the door open so that I could see from the car, she began chasing Irena round the kitchen table with a big stick, landing it across her back now and again. Finally, after being chased round the table for what seemed an eternity, Irena gave up and made a dash for the door and my car. I half expected the old woman to come charging after her, but she thought better of it perhaps. In retrospect, I think the idea of the chase was to force Irena into my arms. I have no idea what Irena's mother was saying to her as the car was stationed some distance from the house, but it could have been along the lines of 'if you can spend so much time with him, why don't you stay with him and do some work,' which wasn't a bad idea, especially as it would soon be harvest time and we'd need a cook (!) at least. As Al Boley used to sing, 'what's to do about it?' I suggested that unless Irena was to return to the house and another bashing, she should come home with me. At least for the time being! Her mother looked after her son which was an idea of her mother's, as she didn't want Irena to bring him.

I had by this time persuaded the Dane who was the Institute's carpenter to make me a double bed, just in case, with book shelves at the back. I had procured a very special double mattress to go on the springs of the bed from another Danish friend, to be paid for 'after the harvest', together with a fridge, a telefunken radio-gramophone, to be paid for 'after the harvest', a table and four chairs and a cottage suite of bamboo which was my pride and joy, also to be paid for 'after the harvest'. I would have to rough it and wait for the wardrobe and dressing table until after the next harvest! We couldn't have everything at once, could we?

We got along very well together, while we had some money, and Irena proved to be a good cook providing for the men and myself, of whom we were now four—myself, Camillo the tractor driver and two labourers, also Italians.

An Italian 'parcelero' sold and erected for me a barn measuring 10 x 20 metres with a corrugated half moon roof and steel pillars in which we put down a concrete floor ready for the rice crop which would be harvested in bags, as there were no drums in those days. The rice would also have to be brought down from Griff's farm, as there was nowhere there to protect it from the rain. Griff had no such thing as a barn. Everything was on a temporary basis with Griff; no long term plan, just here today and gone tomorrow which was one big problem as far as I was concerned.

The barn was to be paid for with the credit received from the Institute for the rice harvest as the flood had reduced my other expenses. I also built a concrete bridge with the help of some Italian labour who were knowledgeable workmen, and a magnificently huge bathroom as an extension to the bungalow with all mod cons, naturally, now that we had water laid on in the house as well as electricity. This and the bridge cost me another Bs2,500 which I paid 'after the harvest'.

We had a lovely time harvesting the 'tronco de cosecha' — tremendous harvest. In Venezuela if anything is exceptionally good it is expressed as being 'un tronco' it being a euphemistic expression, such as 'un tronco de mujer', meaning a lovely woman or 'un tronco de carro', meaning a lovely car. Camillo and I took it in turns on the new combine harvester and on the bags, with the other two collecting the filled bags from the field. On one or two occasions where the ground was soft and wet we had to pull the tractor out of the hole with the harvester. Altogether we harvested 120,000 kilos of rice from the parcela.

Then we moved onto Griff's land. Most of the road to the rice field was just a dirt road and during the wet season it had become full of holes and ruts caused by constant passage of tractors, but we got there all right with the combine dragging anything along behind that wouldn't come of its own volition. I had bought a trailer which had been converted from a lorry and it proved a cumbersome vehicle for a hard road let alone rutted tracks. A smaller trailer would have been more suitable under the circumstances, but we managed to bring the rice down to the barn on my 'parcela' in loads of 80 sacks at a time and eventually harvested another 80,000 kilos. I don't know how true it is, but I've heard it said that farmers only expect to have one good harvest in five. If that is true then this was mine, because I didn't have another one, not a good one.

Before I could sell rice to the private silos, I had to pay off the Institute. So owing them Bs24,000 I delivered 40,000 kilos to the silos in the centre of the Colony and got clearance so that I would be allowed out of the Colony by the National Guard. The next amount to be partly settled was the Massey-Harris distributors in Acarigua, 50 kilometres distant, so I dispatched 75,000 kilos of rice worth Bs45,000, leaving a balance of Bs 25,000. The remainder I sold to a private company in Acarigua which brought me Bs 60,600 to pay the remaining creditors part or all of what I owed them—for the John Deere, the Ford station wagon, the lorry, the household furniture and for the Frenchman's 50 hectares of land. I still owe the Frenchman a balance of Bs5,000 as, being involved with Perez Jimenez's government which was later overthrown, he had to flee the country to escape repercussions of his associations. The same happened to the Italian who deforested the 50 hectares before I could pay him.

By promising to pay the remaining balances due on the agricultural machinery and the station wagon over the next two harvests, everyone was perfectly happy.

After dealing with the rice harvest, Irena and I were invited to Dr Sam and Mrs Weaver's farm, San Jose, on the outskirts of Acarigua. They were Americans who had been working for Rockefeller at Palo Gordo, but were now farming for themselves on a large scale. Irena, who was a clever dressmaker, made herself a mini long before they became fashionable, especially for the party. There were a lot of expatriates there of many nationalities such as Americans, British, and Danes who all spoke English, but Irena felt left out of the conversation and drove off into the night in my new station wagon, returning periodically to see what was going on. But then she didn't return and I became concerned about her welfare, as well as that of my brand new car. She had no licence and wasn't insured to drive it. After contacting the National Guard, I discovered that the traffic police had stopped her for speeding in town and for being over the limit, and had thrown the book at her, putting her in jail for the night. All problems with the Venezeulan police can easily be solved providing you show them the colour of your money.

Once I was driving alone past a police station where there was a lone policeman on duty; he flagged me down and got into my car saying that I had been speeding, which was the last thing you do in Venezuela even if you are driving a station wagon that will do 180 kms an hour. I disagreed.

'Si senor como no. Hay una fiesta esta fin de semana y Ud no quiere estar en preso por el fin de semana, Es mejor que Ud me da una platica para unas cervezas y cigarrillos.' — 'Yes sir, you were. There is a festival on this weekend and you don't want to spend it in jail. It is better you give me a little money for some beer and cigarettes.'

'Como no Senor, pero yo no tengo mas que Bs150.' — 'Why not sir, but I have only Bs150.'

'Esta bien, no importa.' — 'That's all right, don't worry', and I gave the policeman all I had which was the equivalent of £15 and went home because I had no money left.

Fortunately, I had some cash left over from the rice crop and was able to get Irena out of jail the same night. Goodness knows what would have happened to her wearing that mini dress if I had not, but the palms of many hands had to be greased and no doubt the police were able to celebrate that night. Of course, it was my fault for not paying her more attention at the party, but I was enjoying meeting someone of my own nationality, even though she was a Scots lady! Most people at that time seemed to be doing well financially and holding parties. Another party we attended was held by the Dane, Loughenson, and his wife. Everybody wore masks and no one was able to recognise anyone, a most peculiar situation. Irena wore her mini dress and was getting off with everyone. I remembered to take the key out of the ignition that night.

Not long after we had harvested the rice, I received the shock of my life. Camillo had been working on the land on Griff's farm preparing to plant sesame which would have done well on that soil, as it was a lot lighter than on my farm, and one day he came back to say that I was to take all my machinery away from Griff's farm. Irena appeared to be the cause. One day not long before Griff had passed us in the road, stopping to say 'are you going out with that bitch now?' but I didn't think he was going to be as upset as to break off relations with me because he didn't approve of my association with Irena. I can think of no other reason why he should want to break our contract, even though it was only verbal. He spent most of his time in Caracas with his family in any case and should have known better, though it wasn't for me to pass judgment even though he had a wife and four children! Nevertheless, I had to put my foot in it and lost a tremendous opportunity, probably the best I had whilst in Venezuela. At 36 years of age temptations of the flesh were still too strong and once again the opposite sex was my nemesis.

I was left with more machinery than necessary, and unless I could find some more land I had no hope of being able to pay for it. I went to see if I could get some more land from the Institute. When I explained to Dr Branco, the man in charge of land distribution, what I wanted he observed: 'Nosotros no estamos enamorado, Senor Jay' — 'We are not in love, Mr Jay.'

'No Dr Branco, no estamos enamorado, es verdad!' — 'No Dr Branco, we are not in love, it is true,' but there I was lost for words because I had not the faintest idea what he meant. He didn't give me the impression of being queer, so what could he have meant? About 30 years later the penny dropped. One of the problems of being brought up in a family with a Christian background was that before going to Venezuela I had known nothing of corruption. You certainly wouldn't find it in the Grenadier Guards and neither in the field of music, but in Venezuela it was rife. What Branco wanted was for me to share with him the proceeds of the harvest if he gave me some land on which to plant, and there was much available, but I did not understand. I knew a lawyer in Caracas who became the Venezuelan Ambassador to Sweden not long afterwards, and approached him to see whether he could help me in getting some more land, but he wanted Bs20,000 — £2,000 — but I thought that was too much at the time, and that was for a larger parcel of land which I could choose.

The 'parceleros' in the Colony were having problems in being paid for their crops. Payment was slow in forthcoming so some of the more articulate such as Salazar, Giorgio Saopaulo, Renoso, Chacin, Opreshko and Mujica (Venezuelans, Italians and Germans) got together and formed what they called La Associacion de Productores de la Colonia de Turen. This literally translated means The Association of Producers of the Turen Colony, but would be more appropriately called The Farmers Union of Turen Colony. Two more nationalities were called upon to support the committee, a Spaniard by the name of Evaristo Salva and the only Englishman, by the name of Bernard Jay. There was only one person it was considered worthwhile discussing the problem with, and he was Dr Tamayo, the Minister of Agriculture, and to do this we all travelled to Caracas in two cars, mine and Giorgio's (a good friend of mine to this day incidentally, who is still going strong at 70 years of age on his farm). We stayed at the Hotel Comercio in downtown Caracas and the first thing Salva did, being the secretary, was to make an appointment to see the Minister, which he couldn't arrange until a week later. We had only a certain amount of finance available which had been contributed by the members of the newly formed Farmers Union, so could not afford to stay in town for long. We were treading on dangerous ground as the country was being ruled by a dictatorial regime with the little fat man, Perez Jimenez, at the helm and unless we were careful we could land up in the dungeons at Puerto Cabello, especially reserved for political prisoners—in the eyes of some it could have appeared that we were instigating a peasants revolt.

In due course Dr Tamayo granted us an interview and we traipsed along to his Ministry. We were shown into his office, which was more like a conference room, and once we were seated in a row he asked us our names and nationalities, and what the problem was. In one voice we replied: 'Queremos plata Senor Doctor'—'We want some money Doctor' (all big knobs in Venezuela were Doctors

161

of something or other). 'Los parceleros estan muriendo de hambre y tienen algunos muchos hijos' — 'The parceleros are dying of hunger and some of them have a lot of children.'

The Doctor replied 'No se preocupe, mis hijos, el dinero viene ya, puede ser manana o despues de manana' — 'Don't worry, my sons, the money is coming already. Maybe tomorrow, or after tomorrow. (It's always tomorrow, or after tomorrow in Venezuela). Then Tamayo said something that rather shook us: 'Es mejor que Uds., regresan rapido a sus casa porque sus familias van a pensar que Uds., estan preso' — 'It is better you return quickly to your houses, because your families will think you are in jail.'

We returned at once to the Colony with the good news, some of us being greenhorns to the politics of Venezuela, that payment for the farmer's crops was arriving 'tomorrow or after tomorrow' as the Minister had said. Everybody breathed a sigh of relief. They actually got their money two months later, just in time to plant the next crop. Meanwhile the German supermarket and the Italian supermarket in Turen kindly gave the 'parceleros' extended credit, no doubt inflating the prices of groceries so that the poor farmers, as always, were the losers.

It wasn't until a year later that I got another farm of which only 15 hectares had been deforested. By this time I had lost all my machinery and the 50 hectares I had unwisely bought from the Frenchman. As I was not able to keep up the payments on the machinery and car the distributors had arranged between themselves to get me away from the farm on some pretext or other, and descended on the 'parcela' removing everything, lock, stock and barrel, except the implements belonging to the Institute such as the drills etc. Steinforth of Massy Harris summoned me to Caracas to appear in Court, suggesting that I bring a lawyer with me on such and such a date. The lawyer, his brother, and I drove to Caracas in his car and we spent the night in a five star hotel in Los Teques, at my expense, before proceeding the following day to the court, where the lawyer was invited inside and signed away my 50 hectares as well as any rights to the machinery of which I'd paid more than half the cost. No doubt 'my' lawyer was compensated for his treachery by Steinforth, but I didn't see him again that day and had to make my own way home with Steinforth giving me a lift down town and saying in English 'I expect you feel better now.'

The bastard is now dead and he left all his money, including my 50 hectares, to his mistress, upsetting the rest of the family. I met the little son-of-a-bitch of a lawyer a few months later in a bar. He was drunk as a coot and said to me, 'Uds me debe dinero'— 'You owe me some money.' I looked him in the face and walked out without a word. So much for legal chicanery. Unless you can speak Spanish fluently in Venezuela it's better to stay away if you are in business.

The Ford station wagon was also taken away of course. Jose Benitez, who had recommended that I buy a Ford, hoping to get a commission out of the introduction, was extremely angry and filled with incandescent rage one morning when I wanted to have a word with him as I passed his parcela. He was standing outside his shack and as I approached him he called out to his tractor driver, 'Antonio, traiga me la machete'—'Antonio, bring me the machete.' Jose was an obese 45 year old so I didn't think he wanted the machete to start weeding his maize. I walked away. I wasn't prepared to enter combat even if I'd had a machete, let alone being completely unarmed. Because I had not completed the payments for the station wagon Jose did not receive his commission and was slightly put out!

Everything was falling apart. Irena decided that there was no future with me and said she was going to Caracas to stay with some friends, but left some of her belongings in the house. Two months later she returned accompanied by two men; an American and a Venezuelan, to collect her things and asked me if I wanted her to come back. I said no, and that was that. She wrote me a letter six months later wanting to come back, but I did not reply. Goodness knows what she'd been doing in Caracas, but one has one's suspicions.

I wasn't the only person having problems. One friend, Weaver, lost his farm to the Chevrolet distributor because he couldn't pay for his vehicle. Weaver, not being fully conversant in Spanish, had signed away his farm when he signed the contract for the Chevrolet. When the time came to pay his next installment he couldn't meet it because his rice had failed. He lost everything. Another American, an ex-parcelero, sold his farm to a native who paid the first two installments, defaulted on the rest, and kept possession of the farm by some legal chicanery.

It was impossible to farm without machinery and after such a traumatic experience I was in no state of mind to start all over again. It's no use in retrospect saying what I could have done when I held a comparative fortune in my hands. Being a fairly honest person my sole intention was to pay for the machinery, illustrated by having paid completely for some of it, and more than half of what was owing on the rest. Instead, I could have done what a Spaniard did, which was to dispose of the crop once he'd got permission to take the rest of his harvest out of the Colony, go to Caracas and put down a deposit on a new car and drive off down to Chile with the proceeds. I could have driven off in my new station wagon and about Bs80,000—£8,000—which was then a reasonable sum, but I wasn't brought up with that sort of mind. Or, I could have sent the money, which was possible at the time, the banks not asking questions, home to England to buy an 80 acre farm for £100 an acre (I used to read the Farmer's Weekly which was sometimes sent to me). But no, I was honest Joe, which goes back to my childhood upbringing, thanks to my beloved parents. I'd much rather be the way I am, as my Aunt Alice said once of a friend of hers, still 'scrattin to make a livin.'

By some miraculous manoeuvre I salvaged from my piece of land 10,000 kilos of sesame which a friend of mine, Jan, a Hungarian, arranged to sell for me in Caracas at the market price of Bs1 a kilo, prior to me leaving the Colony to set myself up as a teacher of English in Acarigua. I accompanied Jan to Caracas and he brought me the proceeds of the sesame to the hotel where I was staying where I paid him his commission of Bs500. He later sold some maize for a countryman of his who did not accompany him and, after receiving payment, he went on a binge and forgot to hand over the money for the maize. When he'd spent the money and sobered up, he blew his brains out on realising his predicament.

The moral of the disaster which had overtaken me is do not overstretch yourself. I wouldn't say don't buy on credit, because if I had not borrowed the £250 to invest in a tractor, I would not have been given a parcel of land in the Colony of Turen. It was because I was able to say that I was buying my own machinery that I was given a start in farming in Venezuela. What happened eventually was through bad management and being tempted by the flesh, which has been the downfall of many in higher positions than a mere farmer. If I had kept control of myself I could have taken advantage of a tremendous opportunity, but I let it slip through my fingers.

35 years after I left the Colony there are many houses left derelict as the farmers who occupied them have returned to their countries of origin, having failed to make a go of it. But the farmers who struck lucky in obtaining a fertile parcel of land each now occupy as many as four parcelas, with a total of roughly 200 hectares. Touring round the colony on my last visit in March 1991, there were as many as ten tractors and four combine harvesters parked outside one farmhouse. Of course, like many a British farmer, the Italians and Germans have large families and each member of the family can quite easily apply for a 'parcela' and then all live in the same house as one unit. Much progress has been made during the last 35 years, in as much that many 'parcelas' have the benefit of a bore-hole which costs a million bolivars—£10,000—to sink per hundred metres, but is essential for a good crop of rice. This now sells for Bs11 a kilo, compared with the Bs0.60 a kilo in 1955. Jorge, a Lebanese friend of mine who farms privately outside the Colony had a tremendous infestation of rats in his rice whilst I was there, and was busy rounding up a gang of men with dogs and machetes; the dogs would sniff out the rats as well as kill them and the 'obreros' would have a whale of a time joining in. They'd get so much for every tail they could produce. The rats are said to carry a deadly virus for which there is no remedy. 20 people had already

died as a result of being bitten, and it was becoming increasingly difficult to employ men to control the outbreak.

This particular friend was the proud owner of 350 hectares of land situated by the Sarare river with water flowing all the year round and ample supply to irrigate the rice he had planted, which was about 100 hectares. But he was not very well organised. How he acquired so much land I haven't the faintest idea, but he had some peculiar ideas on how to farm it. He kept repeating to me that he was awaiting credit from a bank in Caracas of about three or four million bolivares, but at the same time he was trying to persuade me to lend him around £35,000. He even tried to seduce me by introducing me, a 71 year old, to some young girls, and the next morning brought me some hormone tablets, which I still have incidentally — unused. When this failed he tried to persuade me to rent 100 hectares for 800,000 bolivares, or £8,000 per crop; that is per six months. This was a ridiculous proposition because no one is going to rent land on a six month basis. Instead of getting on with preparing the ground to plant more rice he was messing about building a chicken run for poultry and said he was going to buy some sheep to graze the bit of grass growing along the dykes where the water ran. I suggested that if he imported some camels from the Lebanon he could use them for ploughing up the ground! Jorge had been in Venezuela for 40 years, had married a Venezuelan and had four children, three daughters and a son (two daughters of whom had been killed in an accident whilst travelling to school in a bus), but was still unable to finance a crop of rice. Once he knew that I wasn't interested in putting my hand in my pocket he stopped visiting me in the hotel.

One of my great delights was when I visited parcela 364, my old parcel of land. For 35 years it had been occupied by two Venezuelans who did nothing to it; didn't even live in the house, but the last time I was there it had been prepared for planting. When I approached the new owner with a Venezuelan friend of mine, he asked my friend in Spanish; 'Es Bernardo Jay, no es?' — 'It's Bernard Jay, isn't it?' It transpired that he was Alvaro Barbiero who was six years old the last time he saw me, the son of Victor Barbiero who occasionally gave me a hand, but who was now dead having been knocked over by a drooling lunatic whilst he was changing a wheel on his tractor on the side of the road. Alvaro, having prepared the ground, was now levelling it with a tractor and leveller ready to plant rice under irrigation by pumping water out of the Guamal Canal with a 12" pump and engine. I understand from a fellow founder of the Farmers Union with whom I correspond, that Alvaro harvested 150,000 kilos of rice, 30,000 kilos more that I did in 1956 without irrigation, even though my rice had a good soaking with the flood. Compared with the production of corn in this country it may be nothing to write home about, but with two such harvests in twelve months it can't be bad. Alvaro, who is Italian by birth but Venezuelan by naturalisation, has another 'parcela' of 40 hectares, left by his father, up the road. He had, incidentally, paid 800,000 bolivares 'ingoing' for my old parcel of land, about £13,000 at the present rate of exchange, which included some machinery. The barn which I had bought and erected had been removed by someone to goodness knows where.

Someone I've always admired, because he was such a good mechanic and could do his own repairs—it's no good being a farmer miles away from a mechanic's workshop, unless you are a mechanic—having worked for Messerschmidt in Germany during the war, is Tony Lock. He is a Croatian of German descent whose family emigrated from Germany to Croatia in the seventeenth century, and from what I gather supported Germany during the 1939/1945 war. At the end of the war his father-in-law was ordered to dig his own grave before being shot in the back of the head by Tito's partisans. Tony's wife was sent to work in the salt mines in Siberia before being released into a displaced person's camp in Germany where Tony met up with her, having known her in his childhood.

Tony Lock and his wife went to Venezuela with his parents in 1950 in one of two boatloads brought to the country by Tamayo Suarez, then Minister of Agriculture in the Perez Jimenez govern-

ment, from the displaced person's camps in Germany for the sole
purpose of occupying farms in the Colony of Turen. They'd volunteered to start a new life and had not been forced to go. They had
initially been taken to El Trompillo, an immigration camp, where
they remained for several weeks before being transferred to Turen
where the family, the parents, Tony and his wife, were given one
'parcela' for all the family. Tony found work as a mechanic in a
garage owned by a German. The only problem was that it was ten
miles from the house, so he acquired a bicycle and pedalled to and
from work. For some reason he lost the job and found another in
Acarigua, 50 kilometres from home where, because of the distance,
he had to sleep in a hammock in the workshop and had his meals
prepared by a kindly Venezuelan lady which wasn't entirely what he
was used to. Again he was paid Bs15 a day. How he managed it
goodness knows, but he scraped together Bs2,000 and he went
along to see my old 'friend' Steinforth who happened to be in
Acarigua in the Massey-Harris office. When Tony explained that he
had only the equivalent of £200 and wanted a combine harvester, he
was told 'No hay problema, llevalo uno' — 'There's no problem,
take one', and that was the beginning of his road to success.
Somehow Tony met the Frenchman, Aubery, from Martinique who
owned a a big farm of 5,000 hectares alongside Griff's farm and
began by helping him with the sesame harvest. Tony did as much
work with his combine as Aubery's two combines operated by
Venezuelans and Aubery was somewhat impressed. Tony reckoned
it was the right time to broach the subject of renting some of
Aubery's land and made a deal to rent 50 hectares in return for 25%
of the harvest, adjusted for a contribution towards the expenses
associated with planting and cultivating the crop. But his sesame
crop was invaded by a weed called the 'pica-pica', a nasty stinging
plant. He recruited some 'obreros' at twice the going rate, ensured
that they were well protected by wearing two shirts with long
sleeves buttoned at the wrist and neck, despite the tropical heat, and
with trousers tied round the ankles with pieces of string to stop the
'pica-pica' going up their legs. The crop was successfully cleaned

and later produced 50,000 kilos on tremendously fine soil, making a profit of Bs35,000. Sesame sold in the 50s for Bs1.12, in the 90s it sells for Bs28.00 a kilo. With the profits he bought a second-hand combine harvester and three second-hand tractors. From that point on he never bought anything else unless he could pay for it.

Tony also rented 100 hectares of good fertile land from Griff for Bs200 a hectare per crop, which was less than what he was having to pay the Frenchman. He remained with Griff's land for a couple of years until he did some harvesting for a couple of Venezuelan doctor agronomists who had farms in the Colony, one of whom said, 'Porque Uds. no tiene una parcela?' — 'Why haven't you got a parcela?' Tony remained silent and the doctor remarked that there were only two things that mattered in Venezuela, the Simon Bolivar, (the currency) and 'el compadre', meaning protector, benefactor, friend and old chap (an expression of familiarity).

The doctor said, 'Yo voy a buscar una parcela para Uds' — 'I'm going to find a farm for you', and he arranged for Tony to buy the next door neighbour's farm for Bs10,000 — £1,000 at the 50s rate of exchange. In due course the parcel of 100 hectares was transferred to Tony Lock and he paid the Bs10,000 for what they call in Venezuela, the 'bienhecharia' — the key money or 'ingoing'. It had a house of a sort and Tony and his immediate family of wife and two children were, after six years, able to set up home on their own.

The doctor and Tony became good friends, great compadres going to cock-fights together in the next village, Piritu, but the 'parcela' wasn't a good one — we can all make mistakes — and it only yielded 300 kilos of sesame and 500 kilos of maize to the hectare. Tony was once again on the lookout for some better land. He gave up contracting because he spent so much time chasing people for payment and eventually found some land owned, or rather rented, by three Arabs who couldn't get on with each other, and he bought them out. This was a farm of 300 hectares which wasn't exceptional either, but he farmed it for 12 years until his brother-in-law sold him his farm of 300 hectares which was the best in the state of Portuguese for sesame and maize, yielding 1,000 and 3,000 kilos respectively per hectare. He remained there for 18 years before selling to a German, a friend of mine's son by the name of Weiss, for 31 million bolivars, in stage payments of course, Bs21 million for the farm and the rest for the machinery. Tony incidentally did most of the work on the 300 hectares himself, preparing the ground for planting with a caterpillar tractor and 35" disks, with a set of smaller discs behind with a roller following. He employed a Venezuelan tractor driver who worked for him for 30 years and did exactly as he was told, because Tony more or less looked after the whole family. Between them they prepared and planted the 300 hectares, 660 acres, in a week with Tony on the caterpillar and the Venezuelan tractor driver following with the drill.

Tony had waited six years before he got a 'parcela' in the Colony, but was jolly glad to get out once he had found a better farm. Only once did he attempt to obtain credit with the Institute de Agrario and when he went along to the office in the Colony Centre he was told: 'No hay plata hoy venga la semana que viene'— 'There's no money today, come next week.' He went back the next week and was told 'Venga la proxima semana porque no hay dinero'—'Come back next week because there's no money.' Three times he returned to the office and on each occasion was told to 'come back next week.' Finally he told them 'Mira, cuando viene el dinero Uds saben lo que pueden hacer con el dinero. Uds pueden hacerlo una bola grande y meterla donde las meten los monos los mani.'—'Look, when the money does come you know what you can do with it. You can roll it up into a big ball and stick it where the monkey sticks his peanuts!' He said he never once asked for any more credit in the Colony. Owning his land outside the Colony he was able to obtain credit with the vegetable oil manufacturers when he planted sesame and companies like Protenal for maize.

After doing well on the farm he bought from his brother-in-law he decided to go in for property developing and bought an option of land in the centre of the nearest town, Acarigua, and drew up plans for a block of flats. These were to cost Bs5,000,000, too much money for Tony, but his next door neighbour, who had previously had a cinema and supermarket in Turen, but was now farming next door to Antonio, was prepared to go in with him. It took them ten years to build Residencia Plaza which is situated in Plaza Bolivar — Bolivar Square — in the centre of the town, with shops on the ground floor and three-bedroomed apartments on three floors above, together with a penthouse on the top floor. The shops were all sold for cash, because if they had been let and there were any problems with the tenants it would have been impossible to get them out.

During my last visit to Venezuela in 1991, I was sitting on a bench with a friend in Plaza Bolivar in Acarigua when an old man, who I did not recognise, came ambling by. He was gaunt with white hair and stopped, staring at us. My friend, Alexis, said to him 'Do you know Jay?' in Spanish of course, and the man replied 'Si yo conozco Jay' and I immediately recognised the voice.

'Caramba chico, es Tony Lock' — 'Goodness gracious me, it is Tony Lock.' 35 years is a long time and Tony Lock had changed beyond recognition. He had worked hard, and was also ill with diabetes and had lost a lot of weight. But he recognised me thank goodness, and we had a long talk over a cup of coffee during the next few days. He told me of a farmer who was an immigrant like himself, but of another nationality, who had built himself a number of silos and had become quite a wealthy corn merchant. For some time he had been trying to persuade Tony to sell his sesame to him and he had finally succumbed to his persuasion supplying the corn merchant with several loads, until he suspected that he was being short changed. To make sure that he was not being under-weighed he checked his load of sesame on a government licenced weighing machine in the Colony Centre before taking it to the merchant. His fears were confirmed when he was weighed in with 500 kilos less than the government's machine had indicated, but when he approached the merchant on the subject he denied that there was anything wrong with his machine. Tony had lost quite a lot of money, but there was nothing he could do about it. The merchant is now dead and was not able to take it with him, because there are no pockets in a shroud. He was, however, able to have his last wish fulfilled and was buried in the land of his birth regardless of cost. How many more people had he conned I wonder.

They say 'when in Rome do as the Romans do' and it certainly applies in Venezeula. You have to forget your British reserve; do a lot of back slapping; have a 'compadre' and the Simon Bolivar speaks volumes. What a pity we are here for only a short time of our lives. How I'd love to return and do it all over again, without the mistakes!

14
Profesor de Ingles

Having decided on my future career yet again, I rented a large house in Acarigua which I intended to use as a school in which to teach English. I had some address cards printed with my name and Escuela Ingles—School of English—in large block letters and bought a set of four books called *Essential English* by Eckersley. Then I organised some advertising—on the cinema screen, and by two fellows carrying sandwich boards up and down the streets of of the town and on which was written 'Profesor de Ingles ha llegado en Acarigua para dar clases en Ingles privados o en grupos'—'Teacher of English has arrived in Acarigua to give classes privately or in groups.' I waited with chalk and blackboard at the ready, but no one turned up. Eventually I was approached by two doctors of medicine who wanted me to give them lessons—at home. It turned out that people are not inclined to come to what is literally your home unless your school is licenced by the government, which is reasonable enough. Once I got started several more doctors with names such as Loyo, Gomez, Lairet, Contasti and Sanchez got in touch, all apparently with the ambition to travel and wanting to speak a little English.

As a result of my growing notoriety I was soon teaching in three schools: the Liceo or Lyceum, the Grammar School or Comprehensive; Instituto de Comercio, Commercial Institute; and the Escuela Industrial or Technical College. My pupils in the last two were mostly adults and well behaved, but the children and older pupils in the grammar school were a bunch of tearaways, especially in the fifth grade where one of them must have been a plant as a communist agitator and was really disruptive. Not having had any previous experience in handling such louts I either sent them out of the classroom or made them stay behind writing out 'I am an objectionable little boy and must learn to behave myself' a hundred times when all the other children had gone home. Some of them must have been in their 20s so that the term 'little boy' was rather demeaning.

On one occasion two boys were wrestling in the playground and the police came along and carted them off to jail. It was said that it had been staged purposely to create a rumpus by the communists, and some of the older boys started throwing stones at the police who fired off several shots in the air. The agitators then gathered the children together, collected wood and old tyres and made a bonfire in the street leading to the school, and afterwards proceeded to make political speeches in the school grounds. Somehow or other the authorities put a stop to it, but the school was closed for a month.

This sort of behaviour was foreign to me, but eventually the school opened its doors again and we carried on in the same disorganised way. One or two of the older boys used to bring limes into the classroom and when my back was turned they'd throw them round the room, sometimes landing on my back. The only thing to do was to tell them to report to the headmaster and let him deal with them, because they were beyond me. The ringleader was finally expelled from school by the headmaster which was a lesson to the other brats, most of them being of one parent families without a father.

Besides giving lessons in schools I had several groups who were studying privately with the intention of going on to higher education in Valencia and Caracas, and who had to be fitted in during the evenings as they, as well as myself, were busy at school during the day.

As in schools the world over there were plenty of opportunities for holidays, too many in fact, about three months a year, but the great thing was that they were holidays with pay. On one occasion when a friend and I had returned from a long weekend we found there were three young men sleeping in my bed; my lovely double bed that the Dane had made for me in the Colony. It's still a mystery to me how they got into the house as the doors were locked, or how they had the shameless audacity to get into my bed. One would have thought that if they wanted to have a rest they could have at least gone to sleep on my bamboo suite of sofa and chairs, but no they must have thought we'll go the whole hog while we're about it. Especially as they finished off a case of twenty-four bottles of beer, two loaves of bread and a cooked chicken. When I saw them in my bed thoughts of the massacre in the Colony flashed before me and I imagined they would have been armed with machetes. Not having the courage to approach them for fear of being attacked I called out to Janus, my Latvian friend, who was much more fluent in Spanish than myself, who shouted at them; 'Que estan haciendo aqui en la casa del profesor? Uds, son ladrons y malcriados, vayase a las casas sitienen, antes que nos llamen la policia, disgraciados'—'What are you doing in the teacher's house? You are thieves and ill-bred, go home to your homes if you have any, before we call the police, wretches.'

Of course, they were as drunk as coots, just yawned got up and urinated in the corner of the bedroom before our very eyes. When they had finished they sauntered off without as much as a thank you for the beer and chicken. We escorted them to the police station, but all they got was a warning. The country was no longer governed by Perez Jimenez, and law and order was breaking down.

Despite its problems, Venezuela is a wonderful country and I took advantage to see some of it during the school holidays, travelling to Merida in the Andes in my Volkswagen Beetle. Merida is the capital of the State of Tachira and from there it is possible to go by 'teleferico'—cable car, to Pica Espejo—Mirror Peak, 4,765 metres high, in four stages, changing at each station to another cable car. The highest peak is Pico Bolivar at 5,007 metres. At Mirror Peak there was a restaurant where people were dancing a 'joropo', the national dance of Venezuela. Some of the dancers were collapsing because of the lack of oxygen, but were able to hire oxygen masks from the restaurant proprietor. One young lady had to be carried the last few metres to the restaurant and others were falling asleep because of the altitude. It was the first time most of the people had seen snow and they were having lots of fun snowballing one another.

It was quite an experience, but everybody was relieved to return to town and get their feet firmly planted on the ground. The change in the climate was pleasant for a short while, but it was too drastic for some of us.

The following day I began the return journey and stayed in a little town called Mesa de Esnujagues, still in the Andes. Here I met an American who had left the States when he was 11 years old to go to Mexico with his parents, and had never since returned home, moving from one South American country to another and working for the Creole Standard Oil Company most of his adult life. However, he now had a small hotel as well as organising the local Y.M.C.A. hostel, and was President of the State of Merida's Tourist Association. For 16 years he had been working on a plan for bi-lingual high schools and I hope he was able to achieve his ambition. The Andeans are polite, gentle, soft spoken, respectful and level headed, whilst the people living on the 'llanos' or plains are quick to anger, impatient, loud mouthed, emotional, impolite and in general badly educated. The reason appears to be the difference in the climate. In the Andes it is cool and agreeable, and down on the plains it is hot and dusty. Arne Baxter wanted me to stay in town so that I could help him with the project, but I had commitments with three schools in Acarigua, and had also started to plan a visit the land of my birth, which I had not seen for 12 years, during the summer vacation. Maybe some other time I could help the American out, I told him. I had at least learnt that you never say no to anyone in Venezuela, you never know when you may need to say yes.

Back in Acarigua I sweated from 6 a.m. until midnight in contrast to the lovely climate in Tachira. Acarigua is not more than 400 feet above sea level, if that, and when you go for a walk after 10 a.m. you walk on the shady side of the street.

Another wonderful place to visit was the Island of Margarita, discovered by Christopher Columbus in 1498, some time before I heard about it! It lies 40 kilometres off Venezuela's north coast, not far from Trinidad and Tobago (there are holidays arranged today combining stays both on the island of Margarita and Tobago). The island's tiny capital, Porlamar, was where all the action was, especially the night life which, 30 years ago, was pretty hectic. It wasn't heard of in Britain in those days and about the only people who visited it were the Americans, mostly bachelors like myself. There were lots of bars with beautiful brown skinned girls which reminds me of the words of a calypso I heard in Trinidad:-

> Brown skin girl stay home and mind baby,
> Brown skin girl stay home and mind baby,
> I'm goin' away on a sailin' boat,
> An' if I don' come back trow away dat dam baby!

Now you can fly to the Angel Falls; visit the Canaima National Reserve, home to 14,000 Pemon Indians who will entertain and feed you with chicken and rice at a price; take boat rides through the mangrove trees spotting the flying fish and colourful birds; take trips on the launch which takes you to Cubagua, the island where they discovered pearls soon after Columbus arrived in town; or scoff 'parilla y yuca y beber cerveza Caracas y Polar todo el dia' — grilled T-bone steak and yucca and drink Caracas and Polar beer all day — Porlamar is a free port where cigarettes and rum are cheap. You can also visit La Restinga which, at 25 kilometres in length, is reputedly the longest beach in the Caribbean. When my friend and myself were there for ten days in 1960 we didn't spend much time on the beach; it took us all day to recover from the night before. The night life didn't leave you much energy for the following day on Margarita Island.

When not exploring the countryside, I taught. My most dedicated pupil was a lady in her 50s for whom I had to arrange two hour long lessons every day as long as I remained in Acarigua, except for weekends. She was the wife of an engineer who had escaped with their son from Czechoslovakia, carrying a revolver and a small suitcase containing their bare necessities. They were now in business repairing machinery, had their own workshop and had built their own house after 12 years of hard graft.

They seemed to be thoroughly restoring their fortunes, but it all came to an end when their son became involved in a fracas between two natives over the ownership of some land. The son, who could speak fluent Spanish having arrived in the country as a child and had been brought up in the region, had been contracted to plough some land for the person who thought he owned it, when the other 'owner' appeared, armed with the national weapon, the machete. The discussion regarding the property turned into a serious altercation between the two Venezuelans and the possessor of the machete struck out at the other, almost severing one of his arms. At this point my friend's son thought it was time to intervene, drew his revolver and shot the attacker dead. He gave himself up to the police, probably more for his own protection than anything else, and explained that he had intended only to prevent bloodshed, but that in the heat of the moment the shot had been fatal. Meanwhile the deceased's seven brothers swore over their brother's grave that they would obtain revenge. It cost the father the fortune of Bs200,000 to get his son out of jail, into the boot of his car and out of the country. The son is now living somewhere in Central America with an Indian woman. His children, a son and daughter, don't know where their father is, and he doesn't know that his parents are now dead. A very sad state of affairs.

For some time I continued teaching English to Germans and a couple of Spaniards, one of whom was later burned to death on a ship while anchored in Vigo, north-west Spain. One of the Germans whom I met in 1991 on a recent visit has done exceedingly well despite a heart by-pass in the U.S.A. where the English I taught him came in very useful, from all accounts.

15

I Return to England after Twelve Years

For the first time in 12 years, time and money allowed me to visit the land of my birth, and in 1962 I arranged to fly home. I arrived in Hereford at about midnight on the train from Paddington, and got my poor old brother-in-law, Ellis Whittal-Williams, out of bed to come and fetch me, which could not have put him in a very good mood after slaving all day on the farm. My dear sister, Kay, surprised me next morning by having fetched Mum and Dad who greeted me when I came downstairs. It was wonderful to see everybody again after such a long time. If you are in jail for 12 years you have visits from your family every now and again, but I hadn't seen mine for all that time, nor had it been possible to see them.

During my two months vacation in England I became involved with an old flame of mine, like an idiot. I should have had my head seen to as even before we got married she walloped me round the ear-hole whilst I was driving the car on our way to visit some relatives. She opened the flood gates and with tears streaming down her cheeks begged me to pull into the lay-by. Without explaining the reason she said she was sorry and we kissed and made up, instead of me turning the car round and taking her home to her parents and saying 'Adios muchacha' — 'Adieu girl.' Being the perfect (!) gentleman, and having committed myself, I kept my word and we got married on the understanding that she would be coming with me to Venezuela, but after our honeymoon and when I was due to return she changed her mind. This was perhaps just as well because I doubt if she could ever have adapted to the heat and the complete change of environment, including the language.

If it had not been for my aging parents I would have returned to Venezuela and carried on with my teaching, because at the time I was earning almost £50 a week, compared with the £15 a week I was paid when I returned to England. I had intended opening a government licenced school for English for which there was an opening. As it is, there are now three schools teaching English in Acarigua, but using an Israeli method. How much better it would have been to have had a sign over the school announcing 'Escuela Ingles con metodo Ingles', and with an English Principal, even if he had been speaking English with a Herefordian burr. But no, I, Bernard Jay, had dropped another clanger and had been tempted by the flesh again. What a lot of idiots some men are, but thinking it would have improved the quality of life it was my firm intention to try and meet a member of the opposite sex who would be prepared to 'have a go' in Venezuela.

So I used my return ticket to collect two month's salary from the three schools and settle my affairs; almost giving away my beloved three piece mahogany bamboo cottage suite, Volkswagen car and the rest, and resigning my posts with the schools. As I was not on contract there was no problem in doing that and we parted friends. Indeed so much so that on my last visit, even though the headmaster of the Grammar School had retired, I was still remembered and invited to return 'cualquier dia', any day.

Before returning to England I simply had to say good-bye to my dear ex-stepfather, John Hanson, the Dane, the greatest gentleman I have ever known in my life. As he was the Sport's Club secretary in Baruta, Caracas, at the time, it meant having to stay in Caracas for a couple of days. John came with me to Maiquetia Airport where we had a farewell drink and I missed my plane. The British Airways manager very kindly arranged for me to leave on the next KLM flight.

The first thing one of my new in-laws said to me was 'I expect you've made your fortune, haven't you Bernard?' to which my reply was, 'Yes, and lost it' so that any hopes they had of me buying a farm in the area was dashed to smithereens. The worst thing on this earth is being unskilled. There is no need for it today as we've various training schemes in this country and there is the possibility of everyone learning a trade. It was unfortunate that I did not try to learn something about mechanical engineering when I was in the army and on the transport, but I never had the opportunity, and in any case was afraid of getting my hands dirty!

If you are 43 years of age and unskilled today it is almost impossible to get a job, and it was no easier in 1963 unless you were prepared to do a labourer's job. I was offered work at an army ordinance depot for £9 a week, probably because I was an ex-serviceman, but I wasn't going to be able to live in the style to which I had become accustomed, even though I was assured that there would be opportunities for advancement. Incidentally, members of the chorus in High Button Shoes were being paid £9 in 1948 and this was 1963. Of course, I was very grateful, but I'm afraid the environment did not appeal to me either.

My relatives, namely my brother-in-law and sister, finally came to the rescue and gave me a job sorting spuds and driving a tractor. I remember that as I was so out of condition, having spent time as a teacher, certain people were taking the mickey as I heaved and grunted the sacks of potatoes around.

They also helped me to get a job with an oil company, making cold calls on anyone likely to require fuel oils of any kind such as petrol, derv, gas oil, commercial paraffin and lubricating oils and grease. I found this pretty exhausting as talking to complete strangers wasn't one of my favourite hobbies. One of the jobs I was called upon to do when we were short of a driver was to drive the 4,000 gallon tanker to fetch fuels from Dagenham in Essex. I enjoyed this much more than having to talk to people, but its drawback was that I had to do it at night sometimes after I had been on my rounds during the day, setting off at 7 p.m. and returning at 4 or 5 a.m. the following morning.

My wife and I were renting a farmhouse belonging to my wife's sister and husband and which my wife was using as a Guest House. But as is the wont with relatives, problems arose and we decided to move. My wife and I weren't getting on very well either as the situation had deteriorated ever since the first morning I left to take up my new job and received a clout on the back of the head with the frying pan as I was going through the door. Again this happened without any explanation as to the why or wherefore, just as had happened with the handbag before we got married. When the strange behaviour continued I visited my wife's doctor hoping that he would be able to help me with some advice, but he refused to discuss the problem saying that it might lead to complications should there ever be legal proceedings.

With the help of Hereford City Council, I bought a lovely Victorian house on the outskirts of the city which we furnished by attending the furniture auctions in and around the county. But when this was completed and part of the house redecorated the situation, instead of improving, became worse. There are two things you don't want; a woman who doesn't know her own mind and an ulcer. I had acquired both, and coupled with my job of having to meet strangers all the time, I was a nervous wreck.

One morning when I arrived in the office my boss greeted me with 'Good morning, Bernard, why don't you get your domestic affairs sorted out?'

I countered with 'What do you mean?'

'A Welsh woman rang me up and asked if a Bernard Jay worked for me.'

'That must have been my wife,' I said, 'she's very good at disguising her voice with accents and is a good actress, but she's also stark raving bonkers. I'm sorry she's causing trouble.'

The boss said, 'That's not all, she's been to see the Company's accountants in Gloucester asking questions about you, about how much you earn.'

I assured him that I would have a word with her, but that she would, no doubt, deny all. I also assured him that I knew no Welsh woman, however much I loved all Welsh women.

One morning when I woke up my wife was nowhere to be seen. When I returned from work in the evening, her brother phoned me up to say that I was to go and fetch her from Gloucester railway station at 7.30 p.m. the same evening as she had been to London for the day. She had actually spent the day on Paddington Station being fed tranquilizer tablets by some woman, she told me.

The final crunch came when I was being accused of having affairs with women in the road when I took the dog for a walk, diving in through the back door for a quickie while their husbands were out having a drink at the local. To crown it all, I was supposed to be having an affair with her sister-in-law, which caused an explosion on the Richter scale. I took off to see the relatives, but half way there I changed my mind and when I returned home my wife was on the phone explaining what had happened. In the shake of a lamb's tail her mother, brother and sister-in-law were on the doorstep, her mother exclaiming 'this is Bernard's fault'. My wife sat on a chair and screamed her head off as she had done on numerous occasions previously, but not in the presence of her relatives, as far as I know.

Next day at lunch I thought I'd call to see how my wife was. Her mother had called a doctor who'd brought in a psychiatrist who told me that my wife had accused me of letting women in through the back door at 4 a.m. (Why 4 o'clock? It would have been a bit late, wouldn't it?) which was preposterous. The psychiatrist suggested that she had some treatment, but she refused and her family obviously didn't try to persuade her.

I was too old to join the French Foreign Legion, but the Canadian Immigration authorities were in town advertising for men interested in farming in Canada, so looking for a means of escape from the mess I'd got myself into, I went along for an interview to see what they'd got to offer. It turned out that it wasn't dissimilar to the scheme in Venezuela and, being the everlasting romantic adventurer, I showed some interest knowing full well that a certain person wouldn't have the courage to follow me over there. I assured the official that I would give it some thought and let him know. However, later, in the back of my mind there were my elderly parents, who were about the same age as I am now, very old, as a friend always jokingly reminds me. I'd been reminded on several occasions by relatives since I'd come home from Venezuela that I should be looking after my Father and Mother, or at least be on hand should they need help. The fantasy of emigrating to the wilderness of Canada which undoubtedly it would have been (a friend told me once that before the invention of the tractor you hardly had time to get the harvest in before it started snowing) had to be abandoned. The official sent me a number of missives extolling the advantages of farming in Canada, but he gave up eventually.

Another distributor took over the oil company and for a short while I was employed by the new owner. As they were often short of drivers I was detailed to deliver fuel oils to the customers, until the atmosphere between the transport manager and myself became rather strained. The boss phoned me up one day and said that as there seemed to be a clash of personalities between me and his manager—they'd been together in Italy during the war—I would have to go. Sometime later I was rather chuffed to learn that the manager had been caught fiddling the fuel and flogging it to some other distributor and had got the boot.

Determined to bring the unhappy state of affairs to an end I was to jump out of the fire into the frying pan and bought a franchise by borrowing £2,000 from friends in Venezuela. The following week the franchiser's solicitors wrote to say that the company had gone into liquidation. In the course of time I have repaid the debt to my Czechoslovakian friends.

Having lost the money I had to look for a job and replied to a Nu-Swift advertisement, did a fortnight's course in Wakefield where we were accommodated in one of the finest hotels, and then was allotted the Worcester area where I remained for four months. The company is one of the finest in the country and I would highly recommend it for any young man wanting to start life as a salesman.

Meanwhile my wife and I had parted company, thank the Lord. My father-in-law bought the house from the Council for his daughter, but because I was in so much of a hurry to get away and had no desire to discuss the matter, I ended up forgoing the deposit I had paid and came away with nothing. As far as I know she resides there today, hiding behind the lace curtains.

Two years later we were divorced and she wanted me to pay her a maintenance allowance. I sent the papers to her parents in disgust. She'd got the house, even if it wasn't in her name, and it was furnished with my money. I suppose she thought she was going to sit on her backside for the rest of her life, scrounging off me. As I had left everything to her, her parents persuaded her to drop the claim and I heard nothing more about it. A brother of hers is purported to have said that I only married her for her father's money. Nothing was further from the truth, as the whole purpose of getting married was to improve the quality of life in Venezuela; instead of spending the weekend in the girlie bars I could have saved money and stayed at home!

After four months with Nu-Swift, I branched out on my own. It didn't take me long to figure out that if I was selling fire extinguishers manufactured by Nu-Swift for £17.50 and could buy them for £6 from another manufacturer, I could make 100% profit and compete very favourably with any company. No one was going to become a millionaire selling fire extinguishers these days, but it kept the wolf from the door and provided a living. I proceeded to knock on doors, any door because everybody should have a fire extinguisher and industries need quite a number of different types. I had to keep moving and work an area thoroughly and not have the butterfly approach. Then, once I was in with a supply I followed up with a service and that alone provided my bread and butter.

At the time I was using a typing agency's office as an accommodation address in Worcester. As there was plenty of space, I suggested to the lady running the agency that we could start an Estate Agency from the same office. She agreed, especially as she was only providing the office and I was to do the work. This proved quite successful as it was at a time when property was on the move.

Almost the first thing I did was to put an advertisement in the paper for a three-bedroomed house requiring modernisation and back came a reply, almost by return post, from a couple with a semi-detached cottage for sale in the Malvern Hills; the beautiful Malvern Hills. I went to see it the same day and, subject to contract, as they say, bought it for £2,000, the price the owners were asking. All I had was £200, but it was sufficient at the time for the council to provide the rest. With a grant, I modernised the cottage, building an extension to provide a kitchen and installing a bathroom in the third bedroom. In 1974 I sold the house for £9,750. But then I needed somewhere else to live. I discovered that there was a detached cottage over the hill, only 200 yards away, from which an elderly lady had recently been taken to hospital and that it might be for sale. The sons, after consultation, said 'Yes' and wanted £4,000. Without more ado the deal was made and after much hard work, as I myself was responsible for lowering the floor with a kango hammer, the cottage being built on Malvern rock, it was renovated into one of the most attractive cottages in the Malvern Hills.

My dear little Father came to live with me in that cottage for almost the last three months of his life. Since my Mother's death on 18 January 1965, he had lived with my sister. I was still in business selling fire extinguishers and houses, and came home one day to find that he had a nice bonfire of paper burning in the hearth, not because he was cold, but because he was trying to destroy paper on which he had written something that was illegible. Fearful that he would set himself and the house on fire, I explained to my doctor that I was out all day on business and unable to do my work and look after my Father. The doctor, a wonderful man, came to see Dad and arranged immediately for him to go to hospital where I visited him every night. 18 days after he had been admitted his condition deteriorated, and he asked me to take him home, saying that he didn't want to die there. I was told that the doctor was expected any moment tried to explain that we would discuss it with him, but poor old Dad was very distressed and had much difficulty breathing. A few minutes later the sister arrived and asked me to go to the sitting room and have a cup of tea while they made Dad comfortable for the night. Less than what seemed five minutes later the same nurse came to tell me that Dad had gone to the other side, so something had made him more comfortable very quickly. The sister asked me if I would like to go and see him. He was now on the other side of the ward, surrounded by a screen, still in bed as though fast asleep. He had died in the fourth month of his eighty-fourth year. His father had lived until he was 86. A member of the Apostolic Church who was a great friend of Dad's told me at the funeral that the day Dad died, he had prayed that Dad should go to join his beloved Jesus Christ in whom he had complete faith. His wish was granted, on February 4, 1976.

I sold the cottage later that year for £13,500. My next project turned out to be a house that I bought at an auction for £8,500 which had been turned into flats, two of which were still occupied; one by an old lady and the other by a young couple who were high on the council housing list and left soon afterwards.

The house had been higgledy-piggledy converted into five flats and I decided to change it into four; two up and two down. The old lady was a fixture living in a downstairs flat paying the same rent in 1976 as I had been paying for a flat in London in 1947—30/- a week. I tried to get her other accommodation, not because of the rent but because I wanted to re-arrange the flats in the house, but even by writing to the M.P., Michael Spicer, it wasn't possible.

However, it was possible to convert the rest of the house into three good-sized flats. There was a huge basement, but unfortunately it was impractical to change it into accommodation. There was what appeared to be a fungus creeping up the wall in one of the corners directly under the stairs and foolishly I treated it myself by brushing some liquid onto the infected part without calling the professionals, and forgot all about it, much to my cost at a later date.

The ground floor flat which was completed whilst I was living in it was quickly sold for £9,750, and I moved into one of the upstairs flats which was also on the point of being finished. The two upstairs flats were also soon disposed of, one for £7,500 and the other for £8,750, and not wishing for the grass to grow under my feet having found, at long last, my vocation (!) I frantically chased around looking for a similar property. This proved very difficult, until after many calls on Estate Agents I came across the most magnificent Regency House which lent itself absolutely to five self-contained spacious flats on five floors. The house had been occupied by two old spinsters. Of course, I had to obtain planning permission to do the conversion, but this was done by the architect who had worked on the previous project. It took us 12 months to do the job, travelling as we did for the 15 miles each way picking up the workmen and later the two ladies who did the painting and decorating. People talk of job satisfaction, but no job was ever so satisfying as that was and the flats sold like hot cakes at very reasonable prices. Too cheap in fact. On the down side, I committed one of the most heinous crimes that one could commit without realising what I was doing. I didn't even even appreciate what I'd done until two men had walked by the house some time later and reproached me for it. At the time I'm afraid my reaction was to reply with a mouthful of abuse, telling them to mind their own business, which in fact it was as they were local residents. I had chopped down a laburnum tree to make way for a car parking space. I have been filled with remorse ever since, imagining the colourful display the tree would provide to the local community, though I did plant half a dozen fir trees round the car parking space.

While I was working on the house the lady next door came to ask if I'd be interested in buying hers, which was let into six flats, also in a higgledy-piggledy manner, for which she was asking £30,000. 'Oh' I said, 'I only paid £17,500 for this', and have been kicking myself ever since for not buying it. It was another big clanger I dropped like so many others in my life.

16
The Algarve, Portugal

As I was suffering from arthritis it had been suggested to me that a warmer climate would be more suitable. What they didn't say is that you can't run away from arthritis no matter what the climate is like. However, at the suggestion of my Czechoslovakian friends, I bought a building plot in the Algarve on which I proceeded to build a bungalow, albeit with the intention of selling it.

The Faro estate agents, Oliviera y Viegas, assured me that I would be getting electricity from 'that transformer over there' and that 'all you will have to do is put in about four posts and connect your electricity to the transformer near the restaurant of Alfredo.' When we had finished building the bungalow I approached Alfredo and his response was 'Nao e possivel!' — 'It isn't possible!' After spending most of the afternoon with Alfredo drinking vinho tinto, he promised he would 'falar como chefe do companhia, amanha de manha' — 'speak with the head of the company tomorrow morning.' Alfredo was a builder as well as being the owner of the restaurant, undertaking a lot of work for the council and knew all the right people. But after many afternoons drinking vinho tinto in his restaurant I was no nearer getting the electricity connected. Becoming desperate, I suggested that Alfredo, I and the manager of the electricity company all go out for lunch at my expense. After about six weeks and many more bottles of red wine, Alfredo said that he had arranged a date for the following week and that another friend of his would also like to come for lunch. We duly met at Jose Rivero's in Almancil. The three of them gabbled away in Portuguese during the whole of the lunch hardly noticing me until we had finished and were outside when the manager asked me what it was that I wanted, and I replied 'electricidade, por favor' — 'electricity please.'

'Nao se preocupe, em seis meses voce tem electricidade' — 'Don't worry, in six months you will have electricity.'

'Muito obrigado senhor chefe' said I, 'Thank you very much Mr director.' 'Bom dia e obrigado' — 'Good day and thank you.'

The lunch cost me about £20, but it was four years before I got electricity and it didn't come from the transformer. We had to wait until it came down the road in which we lived which led from the town of Almancil to Vale do Lobo and Quinto do Lago. The estate agents from Faro had dropped me in it once again. For the supply of water we sank a bore hole of 100 metres, which is what most people have to do unless one is on the mains. The moral of the above story is don't buy a building plot unless there is a supply of electricity close at hand.

As a temporary measure I had a generator installed, thinking that it would help to sell the bungalow, but who wants to buy a bungalow with a noisy generator. I soon learned, but it did help me to let it for 12 months via the same estate agents, who were responsible for building a house for their clients and were anxious to find accommodation for them meanwhile.

The bungalow let for £350 a month and I lived in a pensao or pension. I was left to twiddle my thumbs, not even having a garden to tend, and as a result I acquired a taste for the demon drink, red wine, which led me down the slippery slope.

Whilst in Faro I let it slip that I had taught English in Venezuela, and a young girl attending a private school mentioned it to her headmaster who sent for me. I had my four *Essential English* books with me and began to teach in this private school. The Headmaster told me that he had studied at Oxford and was one of the directors of the company which had 20 such schools in the country. I didn't think it was any good telling the headmaster that I had studied in Winforton! Everything was going nicely until one weekend when I went to a night club just outside the town called A

Gruta, the Cave or grotto, and stayed on my own listening to the fados, the popular Portuguese songs, until the early hours of the morning, drinking wine by the bottle. The next thing I remember is walking by the National Guard's quarters and being asked by one of the guardsmen if I wanted to go to hospital, as I had blood streaming down my face. No, I replied I'm all right. I had just been mugged by being hit on the back of my head with something heavy and knocked unconscious, having my keys and money stolen. Having no keys I couldn't go home so stayed in a hotel for the night, being asked by the porter if I didn't want to go to hospital as I was in rather a mess. No, I said, I'll have a wash and go to sleep. The next morning I managed to go to my pensao and stayed in bed for three days. They thought I was a gonner, but I pulled through and reported back to the school, to be met by the director who said you've been here once and collapsed in front of the other directors. You'd better go home and come back when you feel better. Even then I was in no state to discuss the matter or teach, the fact had obviously been playing on my mind that I should have been at the school and had found my way there automatically some time during the last three days, whilst I was suffering from concussion. I'm afraid that I didn't return again. I felt so ashamed of myself and neither did they pay me for the time I had been teaching.

When I went back to my room after spending the night in the hotel, I found that my Grundig stereo radio cassette player and expensive camera had been stolen by the mugger using my keys. My immediate neighbours wanted to know whether I'd had a girl in my room that night as they had heard a man and girl discussing something. I said that no, unfortunately I'd not had a young lady in my room, but that they might have heard two people talking as they had been leaving the pensao with my stuff.

On another occasion after I had spent the afternoon and evening drinking with a Portuguese I had met in a bar, I discovered I had lost my lower dentures which I had the habit of putting in my pocket when I had a sore mouth. The following day I returned to the bar to see if I could find them, and was met in the street by the same

Portuguese, who had been walking up and down the street hoping that I would return. 'Bom dia, Bernardo, como esta voce?' — 'Good morning Bernard, how are you?'

'Muito bem, obrigado, a voce?' — 'Very well thank you, and you?'

'Muito bem obrigado', and then came the sting: 'Tenho suas dentes aqui a quero 1,000 escudos' — 'I have your teeth here and I want 1,000 escudos.'

'Nao tenho mil escudos, tenho so 500' — 'I haven't got 1,000 escudos, only 500', and he settled for that amount. I had had to buy back my own teeth which he had picked out of my pocket.

During some of my more sober moments in Faro I used to go bird watching with a friend, a Doctor Ian Cameron, who with his wife were spending a few months holiday there. He had been a veterinary surgeon in Africa. I think I must have been invited to go with him, not because of my knowledge of ornithology of which I possessed little, but because some boys had been trailing him wanting to use his binoculars which he was not wont to do, believing that once they had hold of them they might run off.

This page: Pied Wagtail; Opposite: White Stork;
p.194: Black-tailed Godwit; p.195: Turnstone;
p.196 Curlew Sandpiper. All drawings by Ian Cameron

Because he refused to let the boys use them, they followed him and threw stones at his ankles, so one day Elizabeth asked me if I'd like to accompany her husband. We spent some very happy 'twitching' together and although unfortunately Ian Cameron is no longer with us, I am sure he would not mind if I shared with you some of the lovely sketches he did of the birds we saw along the coast out of Faro, which he presented to me.

I eventually returned to my bungalow in Vale Verde but by this time I was hooked on the demon drink. I reached a point where I could not sleep after 1 a.m. until I'd had two tumblers of red wine, after which I slept for two hours to awake to find that I had emptied the bottle. Whereupon I'd walk to the taverna, which was just down the road, and wait until Jose opened the bar at 6 a.m. and have a couple more glasses of wine before buying a garrafa—a bottle costing no more than 50 escudos, or 25p, and return home to drink half of it before falling onto the bed completely sozzled. This lasted for about two weeks and made me feel very ill, so ill in fact that I made up a little prayer which was as follows:-

Dear Lord Jesus, please save me from this hell on earth, so that I might be an example to my fellow human beings and a benefit to mankind.

I kneeled on my bed, because of the hard, tiled floor, and repeated the prayer over and over again, before having another swig from the bottle and going to sleep

for a couple of hours. I became so ill that I would convince myself that if I didn't stop drinking I would kill myself. I then stopped for two weeks and when I felt better, started the whole cycle again.

A Portuguese acquaintance once said to me in a bar, 'Voce bebe em excesso. En dois anos voce esta morto' — 'You drink too much. In two years you are dead.' That was in 1983, but thank the Lord I'm still here, because eventually my prayers were answered. Before I left England I had sent off for some literature from the Catholic Enquiry Centre in London, and whilst I was in Portugal I memorised the morning and evening prayers, and used to say them regularly which also helped me to overcome my problem. I'm not a Catholic, but the prayers have been very influential and still are.

Unfortunately the prayers at this stage did not prevent me from drinking. I was driving home one dark night and fell asleep at the wheel, but before the car had collided with anything, it came to a stop voluntarily as my foot fell off the accelerator. I was awakened by a bunch of lads who were helping themselves to my beloved gold ring, watch, any cash that I may have had left, as well as the loud-speakers of the Fiat 127. I remember the boys to this day, because they wore some very strong aftershave which I could smell. However, my eyes were not focusing properly, so I couldn't see their faces and wouldn't have been able to recognise them at an identity parade, except for their colour. Losing the ring was a tremendous loss to me as I had bought it in 1955 in Venezuela, and had had the lion and unicorn cut in to the ring. It was of great senti-mental value.

Another night, driving home from a celebration with an old army acquaintance—I say acquaintance, because although he had been in the same regiment he had not been in my battalion—and his family, I fell asleep and the car crashed into a concrete pillar, somewhat damaging the radiator! I was slightly shaken up, but because I had been asleep I survived unscathed. A kind Portuguese gave me a lift home and the following day I instructed the English mechanic to collect and repair the car, and then sell it to the first person who came along. It had not been the first time that I had had a near shave and the situation was becoming serious.

At the end of every evening I went out to switch off the generator at the villa. One time, as I turned round to leave the generator shed, I was felled with a ladrillo—a building pot, and robbed of 5,000 escudos, about £25. How do I know it was a ladrillo? Because, when I woke up next morning I had a nice big bruise on my chest the shape of a building pot, the sort they use in the Algarve. Thank the Lord for a strong heart, because anyone with a weaker heart would have been killed.

One day when I was going indoors, a fellow who I had never seen before came by riding a motorbike, and stopped to ask me if I was going out that night. No, I said, I was staying at home. The next night, a Friday, I remember it well—it must have been during one of my sober moments — having retired early, I was awakened by a tremendous crash in the bathroom and somebody trying to open the bathroom door. I always locked all doors, especially that to my

bedroom. I grabbed the 18" cold chisel I kept under my bed and, sitting on the side of the bed banging the chisel on the tiled floor, I shouted 'Que quere voce?'—'What do you want?' It was of course obvious what he wanted—anything of value, money or jewellry. I did not know how many of them there were, so I didn't venture outside my room until the following morning when it was light and I could survey the damage. What had happened and caused all the noise was that they, or he, had thrown a big stone through the bathroom window which was then removed—it was one of those windows—and entered through the window frame, but had to return the same way when he discovered that the bathroom door was locked. Before fleeing empty handed, he replaced what was left of the window, which was very kind of him.

I had an English friend who had his own bolt hole near mine, whom I had helped out whilst he was having his own bungalow built and who took me with him when he went into town shopping as he couldn't speak a word of Portuguese. I called on him one day to find he was entertaining a girl friend and he greeted me with 'What do you want Bernard? I'm having my tea, I'll see you tomorrow.' I felt acutely embarrassed, especially as it was said to me as though I was some kind of lackey in front of his bit of stuff. Later that day he came over to my place with some sweet on a plate

as a peace offering and pleaded with me not to mention the incident for fear of his wife finding out. So far I've kept my word, but the incident stands out in my memory.

One day I met a young American couple in the Vale do Lobo holiday complex where we had a few lagers and decided to go and hire some horses from William, who had a riding stable next door to where I lived. You were always accompanied by one of his grooms, usually a young lady. This was sometime in the afternoon during the hottest part of the day. The next thing I remember was waking up on the beach about 7 o'clock at night, not far from the Vale do Lobo bar. I'd fallen asleep on the horse and slithered off it onto the sandy beach. My new friends left me to sleep it off. My first port of call was the bar for some refreshment.

The same William, who like myself enjoyed a glass or two, came over to my bungalow one night when he heard the sound of breaking glass, carrying a metal bar and prepared to confront the burglar. This time it was a false alarm. Two boys from down the road, who'd already been suspected of stealing clothes off the lines in the neighbourhood, had in the afternoon attempted to get into the bungalow while I was out, but had encountered the usual problem after removing the bathroom window, finding the bathroom door locked. They had not been able to replace the glass properly and had left it leaning against the window frame. When I opened the bathroom door, the window, because of the rush of air, had fallen onto the concrete path outside and smashed the glass to smithereens which is what William heard.

On another occasion when William had had a few, he came round to my place seeking the company of someone who could understand him—I comprehend that wives never understand husbands! After I'd agreed with everything he said, he held my hand and proclaimed his love for me. He wasn't queer, he just wanted to talk to someone.

One of my neighbours, who I understand was a Freemason, told me one day when I thanked him for helping me into the house, 'Oh, that's not the first time I've found you lying on the ground inside your drive gate. I've helped you on two previous occasions.' I'd obviously made it as far as the entrance to the property and collapsed comatose onto the driveway, remembering nothing.

My favourite pastime during my periods of sobriety, was to walk down to my preferred spot on the beach some 4 kilometres from the bungalow and away from the masses, and have a swim. One day when I was returning I felt a terrible pain in my left eye, and awoke the following morning with it almost closed. At the time I was painting the garage, but was unable to continue because I lacked the energy and asked a friend of mine, Mario, if he would mind finishing the job for me. All I wanted to do was to lie down on my bed. I wasn't in any pain, I just felt listless. I hadn't the strength to get anything to eat so Mario's wife sent me some soup. I must have been slowly sinking because Mario announced that he was sending for the ambulance. Before it arrived I had become unconscious.

I woke up, or regained consciousness, three days later with a lot of people standing round the bedside. I shall never forget Dr Pinhiero approaching me saying, 'Tudo bem?' — 'everything all right?' He was a wonderful doctor who was attending me in the hospital in Faro, and had been for the last three days. God bless him and everybody in that tremendous hospital. Some foreign countries are criticised for lacking in medical services, but I have nothing but praise for what they did for me. I owe them my life, and to Mario even more so, because if it had not been for his vigilance I would have been a gonner. I remained in the hospital in Faro for three weeks, and left looking like, as they say, death warmed up. I had lost about three stones and looked about 90 years of age but I was, praise the Lord, still alive thanks to everybody. What had happened? Everybody said it was the drink because of my reputation, but I had not had a drink that day. Perhaps it was a viral infection picked up in the sea.

Very occasionally when I'd had a few drinks I'd get it into my head that I'd like to go to the Vilamoura Casino just for a look round and for a drink; I enjoyed the atmosphere and one night I decided to have a go on the roulette table. After changing some money for some chips, I put a 100 escudo chip on number 36, my favourite number. Lo and behold it came up, causing some excitement which attracted the attention of the manager and a couple of 'heavies'. Having been successful with my first bet, I put 200 escudos on the same number, 36, which to my astonishment came up again. Being unable to control my emotions I was practically lifted off my feet and frog-marched outside without my winnings which amounted to over 10,000 escudos, some £500. They didn't even allow me to collect my chips, so I had no claim on the money. I had, however, a few from my first winnings and a lady friend of mine employed by one of the best hotels in Quarteira, the Dom Jose, accompanied me back to the casino the following day. They wouldn't allow me into the Casino, but the young lady was permitted to go through and collected the winnings. Of course, she got her whack for the trouble!

Another diversion of mine, apart from the discos, were the boites. A 'boite' is not a brothel as some would imagine, but a 'rip-off' house where hostesses entertain you to a dance as long as you keep the champagne flowing at £20 a bottle. One night I was persuaded by my partner to provide a bottle of whisky which was fast disappearing when, through the haze, I discovered that the doorman was creeping up behind and helping himself to the bottle. I was rather annoyed he hadn't asked if he could have a drink, but what can you say when the girl accompanying you says: 'Voce nao quere que Manuel bebe tambem?' — 'You don't want Manuel to have a drink as well?' 'Esta bem' — 'It's all right.' As they both lived not far from where I lived I used to give them a lift home. One wanted to be dropped off in one direction and the other in another, and so I thought that they lived in different houses. In fact, I later discovered, Manuel retraced his steps to the apartment building where the girl lived. No wonder she gave Manuel permission to help himself to the whisky and I lost interest in my fancy.

Getting short of cash I relet my bungalow, this time to an English couple who were building a house. I stayed in a pensao in Loule which provided sleeping accommodation only, at a most reasonable rate, but unfortunately across the road there was a bar that opened at 6 a.m. and during my two weeks on the binge I used to look out through the window, waiting for the pub door to open. I reached the stage where one morning my hands were shaking so badly that I couldn't pick up the glass. A kind Portuguese, who happened to be having a drink the other side of the bar having observed my problem, came round, picked up the glass and put it into my hands whereupon I drank the wine in one gulp, stopped shaking and ordered another glass of wine which I picked up myself.

There is no doubt that the worst thing that happened to me during my unfortunate decision to go and live in the Algarve was when my sister and brother-in-law came over from England and caught me during one of my drunken bouts. They were so disgusted they left me to it and made their own way round the Algarve, returning only to say good-bye the day they left to go home. My sister's last words to me were 'have you made your will?' She obviously thought that I was not long for this world, but thankfully, due to no one else but the Lord Jesus Christ and myself, I am still here. When I recovered my composure I was disappointed in myself for not having remained sober long enough to have shown them around the country. The terrible thing was that I knew they were coming and even that did not keep me off the bottle. The way to drink wine, by the way, is with one's meals only.

But my prayers were about to be answered. By the grace of God, and I'm sure that it was through Him, I decided to get away from the environment of the Algarve and go to the Isle of Man for three months. Ian Cameron had suggested that when I sold my bungalow in the Algarve it would be sensible to put the money in a bank on the island where it would not be taxed, until I decided what to do next. It seemed a good opportunity to visit the place, but on the way there I landed up in St Mary's Hospital in Paddington, having become ill with alcoholic poisoning as a result of mixing the drinks. I remember walking into the hospital entrance and saying to the porter that I was feeling very ill and he, with a smile from ear to ear, told me to 'go right through, and they'll put you right.' I felt a tremendous sense of relief—I wasn't going to die yet. The doctor asked me what was wrong, but I felt so ill I couldn't explain what was the matter. They put me in bed and treated me for five days before announcing that I'd got to go as they needed my bed for someone else. I pleaded with the doctor to let me stay for a few more days, but in vain. I think that experience was enough in itself to cure me of my problem, because I had never felt so ill in all my life. I thought it was the end. It was the end of something else, however, and that was the end of my craving for red wine and although I have had the odd glass since, I've now completely cured myself with the help of the Lord Jesus Christ. The day after I arrived in St Mary's a member of Alcoholics Anonymous came to ask me if I needed help. I told the lady, thank you very much, but we'll take care of the problem, the Lord Jesus Christ and myself. I've often had the urge to go to the Algarve for a jolly good booze up, but so far I've resisted the temptation. One day I'll go just to prove to myself that I can live without it. Like my little Dad used to say so very often, thank you Lord Jesus.

I had to call on my solicitor in Worcester to sort out a few problems and thought I might be able to stay with relatives in Herefordshire for a short while. One thing you have not got to do is go near certain relatives if you are a suspect drunk, because they will tell you to buzz off. I nevertheless did stay with one of my two nephews, for which I was eternally grateful, before I was able to resume my journey to the Isle of Man.

During my sojurn in the Algarve, problems had been brewing in the house in Malvern where the old lady had her flat. The dry rot which I had only painted over had by now crept up the stairs, and the lady tenant in one of the upstairs flats had been driven to sort out the problem herself, as the stairs were in danger of collapsing. I have never in my brief experience of property developing come across anything like dry rot, and had not expected that it could spread so quickly. Having treated it with Cuprinol I thought that it was eradicated, but was entirely mistaken. You cannot treat dry rot simply by brushing the chemical onto the infected part. You have to call in the professionals which is what the lady upstairs did, much to my expense. It cost me £6,000. The estimate wasn't even sent to me and the bill was sent to my solicitor. The lady, vicariously, had also sorted out the problem of the old lady, then in her 80s, occupying the flat on the ground floor. Because her route to the bathroom had been cut off with having the floor boards taken up, the council were now forced to provide the old lady with alternative accommodation. I was now able to modernise the flat and sell it, which just about covered expenses. It's not the job of Estate Agents to tell you that a property they are selling has dry rot, but they could at least once they've sold it to you whisper in your ear that you have something that needs attending to right away. After all they are surveyors by profession, and the same Estate Agents sold the flats for me.

Back in the Algarve, my next door neighbours decided they could now buy my bungalow as it had electric light, and rather than bury their money in the garden it would be wiser to invest it in property that they could let to the tourist trade. They were already letting their villa next door.

For the past ten years I had been suffering from an arthritic hip, and whilst in Hereford had visited a surgeon for an examination and estimate for a private operation, as I was not prepared to wait for two years to have it on the NHS. The cost was to be £2,800, which included hospitalisation in the Nuffield. I thanked the surgeon and said I'd let him know.

As soon as it was possible I made arrangements to see another surgeon, and three weeks later had the operation for a hip replacement for about £1,500, including bed and board in a private room, in one of the finest hospitals in the world in Douglas, Isle of Man. I also had another operation three months later for something else, so that I had two ops for the price of one in England.

17
Wales

Some months later, after recuperating from my two ops, I decided to try my property luck in Wales. It took me some time, but eventually I found a suitable building in the lovely market town of Llandeilo. Overlooking the river Towy, the town lies in the ancient Borough of Dinefwr, once a stronghold of Welsh princes, that has left it with a fair legacy of outstanding monuments, including four historic castles; a ruined but beautiful abbey and mines at Dolaucothi where Romans in A.D. 80 are said to have searched for gold. With the famous Black Mountains in view the Borough of Dinefwr extends over some 374 square miles and in some of the most beautiful country in Wales. The Borough is also a 'twitchers' paradise with the rare red kite having been taken as the Borough's motif. Peregrine Falcon, Merlin, Goshawk and Osprey are resident at times. Greenland Whitefronted Geese visit the watermeadows of Dryslwyn and Dinefwr in winter, together with Bewick and sometimes Whooper Swans. Great Crested Grebe nest at Talley Lakes. During the summer there is a migration of Pied-Flycatchers, Redstarts, Tree-Pipits, Light Ringed Plover and Wood Warblers.

It was in this fabulous environment that I came across a very attractive house with a big crack down one end, so that it was not possible for anyone to obtain a mortgage as it was. It was just what I had been looking for, something to do up. I put some concrete lintels in the wall to stop it from falling apart and refurbished the house, installing an additional toilet downstairs with a shower, and sold it twelve months later making a small profit!

My next project turned out to be a disaster in my opinion, although I didn't lose any money. I bought a building plot, together with eight acres, for £29,500. Then, instead of going round half a dozen builders for estimates, I contracted two builders who provided the labour, but not the materials, partly on the recommendation of the bank from which I obtained the necessary loans. We built a three bedroom luxury bungalow with two bathrooms, one of which included a Jacuzzi. It had fitted wardrobes in all three bedrooms, a fitted kitchen, an inglenook fireplace in the living room and was carpeted and curtained throughout.

The day after selling Ty Grenadier, which is what it was called, Ty meaning house, I was informed that there was a building plot which had just come onto the market that morning, in a most delightful little village of 62 souls only a mile and a half from Llandeilo, which I visited promptly and purchased — the plot, not the village — subject to contract.

This time I was determined to keep down the cost so obtained an estimate from a supplier of timber-framed houses, thinking that they would be more competitive, but at £27,500 for a two bedroom bungalow it was more expensive than a traditionally built bungalow of the same size. This time I had no intention of suffering a bank interest bombshell! But the only way you can really economise is by being able to do most of the work yourself, like my builder of the moment who was introduced to me by a kindly neighbour. He is now on the point of completing the work as I am in finishing this book, which I have been able to write with a typewriter perched on my knees in the caravan in which I have been living. All I have had to do is watch it going up and sign the cheques. It's taken a bit longer than anticipated, eight months rather than three as stated by the builder, but they all say the same — how often has anyone seen a house built in three months? The trouble with builders is that they are like a lot of magpies and try to keep three or four people going at the same time so that they have somewhere to go on a wet day. But I know that I could not have done anything without them, because it is as much as I can do to operate a cement mixer.

Where next? Quien sabe!—who knows. When I was in Venezuela recently, I mentioned to a German friend that I would like to go and live in Brittany, eat oysters and lobster, grow artichokes and cabbage and promenade avec les mademoiselles. He responded with 'you mean you would like to die in Brittany?' Maybe so, but I've still got itchy feet at nearly 77 years of age.

Da boch chi—Good-bye.

Appendix
The Grenadier Guards

In 1656, during his exile in France and Flanders after his father's execution and his own defeat at Worcester, Charles II raised a regiment from among his own fellow exiles which he called The Royal Regiment of Guards. This unit, under Lord Wentworth, fought for Charles against Cromwell's English Army at the Battle of the Dunes, near Dunkirk, France, on 24 May 1658. Charles and his allies were defeated, but after Cromwell's death a freely elected Parliament voted for the restoration of the monarchy and Charles returned to England and his throne in 1660. Doubtful of the loyalty of the army he found in England, Charles and his advisers decided to disband it, but for his personal protection he commissioned Col. John Russell to raise another regiment consisting of twelve companies, the first of which was to be called the King's Company, a title which survives to this day.

Wentworth's Royal Regiment of Guards which had been left in Flanders was recalled to England in 1664, and on the death of its Colonel the following year, was merged into Col. Russell's Regiment with an establishment of 24 companies under the title of the King's Regiment of Foot Guards, commonly abbreviated to First Guards.

The regiment is in the proud position of being the oldest permanent regiment in the service of the King (the oldest regiment in the service of the country is the Coldstream Guards). The Grenadier Guards is, therefore, the senior regiment of the Brigade of Guards and always stands on the right of the line.

The King's Company, which formed part of Russell's Regiment in 1660 has remained in being ever since without any intermission and is formed of the tallest men of the regiment. This company invariably attends the Sovereign within the precincts of Westminster Abbey at the Coronation, and accompanies his or her remains to their last resting place, on his or her death. The King's Company is the only Company in the British Army still to carry its own Colour on parade. The close connection with the Sovereign is further indicated by the fact that its facings have always been in blue, the distinction of a Royal Regiment, and the Royal Cypher has always been borne on the King's or Queen's and Field Officer's Colours. Both King Edward VII and King Edward VIII started their military careers in the Grenadier Guards.

Owing to the fact that they were formed from the joining of two complete regiments, the First Guards have, until fairly recently, always been the strongest regiment of the brigade. The regiment has had three battalions ever since this structure became general and in the Great War, World War One, it had four service battalions. At the time of writing it has only two.

The Third Battalion Grenadier Guards was, until 1919, the only battalion of Foot Guards entitled to march through the City of London with bayonets fixed and colours flying, this privilege having been granted in 1680 owing to the fact that the companies which subsequently formed this battalion were allowed to recruit in the City. In 1919 the privilege was extended to all battalions of the Grenadier Guards.

In commemoration of the defeat of the Grenadiers of Napoleon's Imperial Guards at Waterloo the title of Grenadier Guards was conferred upon the regiment in 1815.

Badges and Colours

The first badge is the Royal Cypher (E.R.) reversed and interlaced surrounded by the Garter (Honi soit qui mal y pense) and surmounted by the Imperial Crown. The Cypher (or initials) is that of the reigning sovereign and changes with each reign.

The second badge is the Grenade which came into use when the regiment received the title of Grenadier Guards in 1815. The Grenade had 17 points to the 'fire' and in the cap badge of the Gold Sergeant upwards the Royal Cypher is embossed.

On the officers' sword hilt is embossed a device including the Rose, Thistle and Shamrock, while these national emblems of England, Scotland and Ireland are also to be found on the King's Company Colour.

From time immemorial, flags, or as well call them now Standards, and colours have been the rallying point in battle. Round them men of all ranks fought to the last and, if need be, died. It was a disgrace for the Colours to fall into the hands of the enemy. In consequence, national and regimental honour became, so to speak, enshrined in the Colours.

Colours are, then, the symbol of the honour of the King or Queen, our country and our regiment, and as such are held in the greatest possible respect. They are, moreover, consecrated before being taken into use. Colours, therefore, receive the highest compliments (*e.g.* the 'present' when the troops are armed) and invariably are accompanied by an escort. Men must always stand to attention and salute (unless under someone else's command) when the Colours pass by or come onto parade.

The foregoing had to be studied and memorised before we left the depot at Caterham, along with the battle honours.

It wasn't surprising that with threats of having to forfeit our weekends and all the delights that went with them (!), we gradually absorbed these, and during the Shining Parades were able to spit out the names and years of certain battles when questioned by the Squad Instructor, who would walk up and down the length of the barrack room inspecting our kit as it was being polished, and fire a question such as 'Where did the Battle of the Somme take place, and in what year?'; 'When was the title "The 1st, or Grenadier Regiment of Foot Guards" presented to us and why?' If you didn't know, instead of being able to go to the N.A.A.F.I. for your tea and wad, Frankie would make you write out the answer 500 times, so that you'd be having nightmares about the Battle of the Somme or Waterloo, especially of the Grenadier Guards defeating the French Imperial Guards at the latter.

Principal Campaigns and Battles

1680-3	Tangier
1685	Sedgemoor
1691-7	Flanders
1692	Steenkirk
1693	Neer Landen
1695	Namur
1702-13	Flanders & Germany
1704	Schellenburg
1704	Blenheim
1704-8	Spain
1704-5	Gibraltar
1705-6	Barcelona
1706	Ramillies
1707	Almanza
1708	Lisle
1708	Oudenarde
1708	Ghent
1709	Tournay
1709	Malplaquet
1710	Menin
1710	Douai
1729	Gibraltar
1742-7	Flanders
1743	Dettingen
1745	Fontenoy
1745	Jacobite Rising
1747	Val
1758	Cherbourg
1759-62	Germany

1762	Denkern
1762	Wilhelmstal
1776-81	North America
1776	Brooklyn
1777	Brandywine
1777	Germantown
1778	Freehold
1781	Guildford
1793	Farmars
1793	Valenciennes
1793-5	Flanders
1794	Cateau
1799	Helder
1799	Crabbendam
1799	Bergen
1799	Egmont-op-Zee
1799	Alkmaer
1806-7	Sicily
1808-14	Peninsula
1809	Flushing
1809	Corunna
1811	Barossa
1813	St. Sebastian
1813	St. Marcial
1813	Nive
1813	Nivelle
1814	Bayonne
1814-15	Netherlands
1814	Bergen-op-Zoom
1815	Quatre Bras
1815	Waterloo
1826-7	Portugal
1838-42	Canada
1854-5	Crimea
1854	Alma

1854	Inkerman
1855	Sevastopol
1882	Egypt
1882	Tel-el-Kebir
1885	Suakim
1898	Khartoum
1899-1902	South Agfrica
1900	Modder River
1914-18	First World War

Battle Honours selected to appear on the colours:

1914	Marne
1914	Aisne
1914, 1917	Ypres
	Loos
1916, 1918	Somme
1917, 1918	Cambrai
1918	Arras
	Hazelbrouck
	Hindenberg Line
	France and Flanders

1939-45 Second World War

Battle Honours selected to appear on the colours:

1940	Dunkirk
	Mont Pichon
	Nijmegen
	Rhine
	Mareth
	Medjez Plain
	Salerno
	Monte Camino
	Anzio
	Gothic Line